Recreating
the American Home

The Passive House Approach

by Mary James

Layout and design: Leanne Maxwell
Copyediting: Irene Elmer

Published in 2010 by Low Carbon Productions
www.lowcarbonproductions.com

This book is printed on 100% post-consumer recycled paper that is acid free and has Eco Logo and FSC certification.

ISBN 9780615397900
Library of Congress Cataloging-in-Publication data available.
Printed in Canada

For Robin and Molly, in the hope that this book will inspire a better future for their generation.

Table of Contents

Foreword

As I begin this foreword, I am traveling back to the United States from the 14th Annual Passive House Conference, held in Dresden, Germany. Reflecting on the experience, I am struck by the momentum that the Passive House (PH) movement has gained and the dedication of those who are actively spearheading its progress. With more than 52 countries represented, it is clear that awareness of the PH approach has spread globally.

For many of us building practitioners, the concept of an affordable very low-energy building has been the Holy Grail. The PH approach is quickly becoming recognized as a consistent means of achieving this ideal. In a nutshell, the PH approach is a reproducible method of creating very low-energy structures at an affordable cost—and this method does not dictate materials, forms, or any of the things that would prohibit its implementation within varied cultures or climate zones.

To become certified as a PH, a project must meet three criteria that are designed to address energy use and the occupants' health and comfort. But the implementation of the PH approach does not mandate that the project be certified. In fact, fewer than 10% of PH projects worldwide have been certified. (And not all PH projects are houses; there are more than 100 commercial PHs.) Whether certified or not, all PH projects are modeled using the Passive House Planning Package (PHPP), a software tool developed in 1990 by Dr. Wolfgang Feist, the founder of the Passivhaus Institut (PHI).

The PHPP is the backbone of the PH approach. For 20 years this software has been used to predict energy use in a PH, and subsequent monitoring of a sample of PH buildings has confirmed the accuracy of this tool. These buildings demonstrate that an initial investment in energy efficiency—thoughtful design and construction of the

Jonah Stanford of Needbased, Incorporated, is the president of the Board of Directors of Passive House Institute US.

thermal shell—allows for significant simplification of the mechanical systems that provide heating, cooling, and ventilation. The cost savings from downsizing these systems help to counterbalance the initial investment in efficiency. The simple, yet profound, concept that it is cheaper to conserve energy than to generate it is fundamental to the PH approach. This affordability element provides the critical tipping point toward mainstream accessibility that the PH approach is now experiencing.

The United States has long held the dubious distinction of ranking high among the countries with the highest energy use per capita. As more and more societal problems are linked to energy use, as our population continues to grow, and as the moment of peak oil production occurs, this is not a title that we can afford to maintain. From environmental concerns to financial stability, the reasons why we need to act now to conserve energy—or more accurately, the negative consequences of inaction—are quickly becoming more evident in our everyday lives. The PH method brings a realistic and quantifiable approach to energy conservation within our built environment that has struck a chord with North American building practitioners. This rising interest is reflected in the growing numbers of trained PH professionals and PH projects here in the United States. At the end of 2008 there were approximately 20 certified PH consultants in the United States. Today there are more than 160 certified consultants. When *Homes for a Changing Climate*, the first book documenting North American PHs, was published in 2008, there were 3 PHs completed, with 3 more under construction. Two years later there are 16 completed, 15 more under construction, and another 40 currently under review for certification by the Passive House Institute US (PHIUS), the nonprofit whose mission is to provide technical support for PH projects. Under license from the PHI, PHIUS serves as the certifier of PH projects and PH consultants in the United States. It has been largely through this organization's dedication that the PH approach has reached the current level of awareness in North America.

As the number of PH consultants has grown, so has the general recognition of the PH approach, as they bring their knowledge back to their communities. Today there are five local organizations supporting the promotion and construction of PHs across the country. In the spring of 2010, PHIUS founded the Passive House Alliance (PHA) in order to support these local chapters. The PHA is now a national membership-based trade organization whose mission is to support local and national PH initiatives in the United States through education and promotion. PHA membership is open to all who are interested and provides a mechanism to be involved in, and educated about, the PH

movement on a national level. The PHA promises to be a place where builders, consultants, manufacturers, and homeowners alike can go for resources and reliable information.

A similar alliance, the International Passive House Association (IPHA), was launched in spring 2010 by the PHI in response to PH construction spreading from Western Europe to the Baltic states, around the Mediterranean region, to Japan, and beyond. Membership in the IPHA allows access to the online information exchange site Passipedia. The Passipedia Web site contains only vetted information and should be a powerful tool for providing information on a construction approach that often strains the traditionally understood limits of conservation.

The recent growth of PH in Europe has been aided by manufacturers who recognize the opportunities inherent in the PH market. Heating and ventilation systems designed to meet very low loads at very high efficiencies, high-performing windows and doors that significantly outperform North American products, and even entire PH wall assemblies ease the fabrication of PH buildings. The lack of access to the right equipment and materials is a difficulty faced by the builders of most of the projects in this book. But I am convinced that this is a temporary difficulty. I am confident that soon we will see American and European manufacturers struggling here for market share of components that are designed for low-load buildings.

I would say that questions related to culture and community present more-complicated obstacles. Fundamental to PH design is the understanding that the thermal dynamics in a structure can be different from what we have become accustomed to. Where typical construction relies on using a significant amount of energy to move heat quickly from one area of a structure to another before the heat is lost though a porous building envelope, in a PH the quality of the thermal envelope is improved to the point that a house can be kept comfortable primarily by relying on radiation and conduction. Energy does not need to move quickly around a house, because there is very little heat loss. In many PHs, a single-point

The concept of an affordable very low-energy building has been the Holy Grail. The PH approach is quickly becoming recognized as a consistent means of achieving this ideal.

heat source can maintain comfortable temperatures throughout the house—a possibility that is difficult to accept for many in the construction and building science industries here. In Europe, a major selling point for new PHs is not the low energy use, but rather the comfort that these homes provide.

However, no myopic approach to reducing the environmental impact of construction will be truly successful. The PH approach is focused on energy efficiency, and does not directly consider the environmental impacts of the construction materials. The widespread use of materials that are petroleum based or require high levels of refinement can quickly undo the best intentions. Weighing these impacts is a balancing act that isn't simple, but it can't be ignored. I would add yet another layer of complexity to this balancing act. We would be remiss not to address concerns related to the greater built environment. How far should family members have to travel to meet such basic needs as earning a living, shopping, or pursuing friendships? Today, architecture that addresses singular client needs is insufficient. A successful project is one that addresses far more than aesthetics and square footage; it must respond to and respect the larger built, social, and

economic environment in which it resides. These are not limitations, but opportunities to contribute to successful communities.

The current economic downturn has had a significant impact on construction and development in the United States. It has had a devastating impact on many communities and families. However, it also has inspired greater consideration of the value of long-term investment, stability, and happiness. Increasingly, in my own practice, I see clients reach the conclusion that expense without value is unacceptable. There can be no better moment for the PH approach to gain a foothold in the United States. It represents a viable, tested method of developing low-energy structures that reflect the new trend toward financial and environmental sustainability. We now know how to do it; it only remains for us to implement it. To quote Dr. Wolfgang Feist, "There is no more trying, just doing."

Jonah Stanford
President, Board of Directors
Passive House Institute US

CHAPTER 1

What Is a **Passive House?**

The Passive House approach to designing, building, or retrofitting homes and commercial buildings ushers in a means of predictably creating very energy-efficient buildings. First implemented in Darmstadt, Germany, in 1990, this method can yield dramatic savings—up to 90%—in heating-and-cooling energy use. In fact, the term Passive House (PH), or Passivhaus in German, derives from the fact that homes built to this standard in Germany require so little energy to heat that a conventional heating system can be eliminated.

Instead, these homes can be kept comfortable primarily through a combination of passive heating sources: heat given off by people, lights, and appliances; sunlight streaming through the windows; and passively warmed fresh air, which is supplied by a mechanical ventilation system equipped with a heat recovery system. Exactly how a house can be kept comfortable while using very little energy to heat or cool will vary depending on the local climate. PH is not a prescription—it is an approach to building that incorporates a thorough understanding of building physics.

The PH approach is practical and has been tested in the field in many and diverse climates, from Sweden to Australia. In Europe, tens of thousands of buildings have been built or remodeled using the PH approach. Now this approach is taking root in American soil. To date, about 70 homes in the United States have been designed or constructed to meet the PH standard.

The beauty of the PH standard lies in the way it combines simplicity and precision. To be certified as a PH, a new home or building must meet just three criteria:

- It must use no more than 15 kilowatt-hours per square meter (kWh/m^2) per year for heating or cooling. This is the equivalent of 1.4 kilowatt-hours per square foot (kWh/ft^2) or 4.8 thousand British thermal units per square foot (kBtu/ft^2), per year.

- Its total primary or source energy consumption— that is, the energy generated at the power plant to meet all of the building's energy needs—must not exceed 120 kWh/m^2 (11.1 kWh/ft^2 or 38 kBtu/ft^2) per year.

This Passive House kindergarten in Heidenau, Germany, which houses 72 children, was designed by Olaf Reiter.

- It must be tested for airtightness and shown to be at a maximum of 0.6 air changes per hour at 50 pascals (ACH$_{50}$).

To be certified as a PH, a retrofitted home or building must meet a similarly brief set of criteria:

- It must use no more than 25 kWh/m^2 (2.3 kWh/ft^2 or 8 kBtu/ft^2) per year for heating or cooling.

- Its total primary or source energy consumption must not exceed 120 kWh/m^2 (11.1 kWh/ft^2 or 38 kBtu/ft^2) per year.

- It must be tested for airtightness and shown to be at a maximum of 1 ACH$_{50}$.

That's the simplicity of the PH standard. The precision comes from the modeling required to calculate the home's energy use with the modeling tool developed for this purpose—the Passive House Planning Package (PHPP)— and the exacting implementation of all of the construction specs. The PHPP is an extremely detailed multipage Excel spreadsheet created by the Passivhaus Institut (PHI). The PHI was founded in 1996 in Darmstadt, Germany, by the renowned building physicist Dr. Wolfgang Feist to research and certify PHs and PH components. The findings from that research were used to refine the PHPP so that it could predict a building's energy use with great accuracy. The PHPP is very useful as a design and modeling tool, because it integrates the local climate data and the impact of every element of the building that affects energy use, such as the construction of the walls, the type and placement of the windows, and the sizing of the ventilation system. Using the PHPP, an architect or PH consultant can quickly see the impact of any contemplated design change—such as, for example, altering the placement of a single window in a single wall—on the building's overall energy use.

The precision needed to complete a PH also depends on the meticulous execution of the construction specs. In order for a building to meet the airtightness requirement, for example, the construction supervisor must be thoroughly committed to quality control on the job site. Creating a continuous air barrier can be challenging enough in a construction drawing, but ensuring that the air barrier is implemented correctly on site by everyone who works on the building poses a whole other set of challenges.

Chris Benedict is the architect of this 24-unit Passive House apartment building being built in Brooklyn, New York.

Constructing a PH requires putting the following principles into practice:

- Superinsulate the entire envelope of the building—walls, roof, and floor or basement. The level of insulation will depend on the local climate.

- Eliminate thermal bridges, or areas with relatively higher thermal conductivity than surrounding areas. Thermal bridges provide easy pathways for heat loss in a structure. They can also cause moisture problems if warm, moist air condenses on a cooler surface.

- Create an airtight structure. A continuous air barrier layer around the entire building envelope reduces the need for heating and cooling, eliminates drafts, and makes the building more durable.

- Specify mechanical ventilation with heat or energy recovery, depending on the local climate. Supplying fresh air and exhausting stale air in specified volumes provides for excellent indoor air quality (IAQ) in a home. Efficient heat or energy recovery is essential to reducing a home's overall conditioning energy use.

- Install high-performance windows and doors. Well-insulated windows and doors that seal tightly are

now available. Their use significantly reduces thermal losses through the building envelope and makes the home more comfortable.

- Minimize energy losses and manage energy gains. Designers of PH buildings must assess how much various factors—including the local climate, available solar resources, window placement, and more—will affect the energy balance in a home.

- Use the PHPP for energy modeling. As I described above, the PHPP is a precise tool and an invaluable aid when designing a PH.

Actual energy use data from the first couple of PHs built in the United States show that this method can be successfully applied in this country. In 2003, German-born architect Katrin Klingenberg built her own PH, the Smith House, in Urbana, Illinois. Monitoring devices installed at the Smith House have demonstrated that the house's performance is consistent with the predicted modeling results. The house uses only 11 kWh/m^2 (1 kWh/ft^2 or 3.5 kBtu/ft^2) per year in heating energy. In 2007, Klingenberg cofounded the Passive House Institute US (PHIUS) with PH builder Mike Kernagis to disseminate information about, and promote the construction of, PHs in this country.

In 2006, Stephan Tanner, a Swiss-born architect, oversaw the construction of a certified PH that he had designed, the BioHaus, a residence and classroom for the Concordia Language Villages, in Bemidji, Minnesota, an area with a very challenging climate. For the last few years, the BioHaus has been using on average 12,000 kWh of electricity per year to meet all of its energy demand. With 402 m^2 of floor area, this translates to about 30 kWh/m^2 annually, or roughly 90 kWh/m^2 per year in source energy consumption. That is 20% less than the modeled consumption, using the PHPP, of 38 kWh/m^2 annually. As Tanner says, this proves that it is possible to meet the PH standard even in one of the harshest climates in the continental United States. Since it is technically feasible to improve a building's energy efficiency by 80% or more while simultaneously improving comfort, and since it doesn't cost

Ranch houses, brownstones, low-income housing, apartment buildings—all of these and more have been constructed to meet the PH standard in climates that range from hot and humid to extremely cold.

much more to do so, Tanner says he has just one question. Why aren't we doing this 100% of the time?

There are many ways that Stephan Tanner's question could be answered, and many reasons why PH construction here lags behind PH construction in Europe. One reason it is harder to construct a PH in the United States is that some of the newest generation of very efficient building components and appliances—many of which are designed in Europe—are not available in this country. In Europe, access to these products, including those that are PHI certified, streamlines the process of constructing a PH. This advantage is evident in the Solar Decathlon, an international competition organized by the U.S. Department of Energy (DOE) that is held every other year. Twenty university-sponsored teams design cost-effective energy-efficient, solar-powered homes and construct them on the National Mall in Washington, D.C. Entrants are judged in ten categories, including design, comfort, and energy efficiency. The winner of the 2009 competition was a team of students from the Technical University of Darmstadt with a PH-designed entry, the surPLUShome. This same team won the Solar Decathlon in 2007. New to the 2009 competition was the net metering category, in which students were challenged to generate more energy than would be needed to power the house. Team Germany won in this category, as well as in the comfort zone category, for maintaining consistent temperatures between 72°F and 76°F and a relative humidity that ranged from 40% to 55%.

The energy not used by the surPLUShome was critical to its first-place win in the net metering competition, and the construction of the highly efficient building shell contributed greatly to this win. The windows, which were manufactured by ENERGATE, had to meet some very stiff requirements, according to Mathias Häußler, head of ENERGATE's Department of High-Insulation Construction. On the one hand, they had to extend

This small home is an affordable Passive House rental unit in western Marin County, California.

visually the interior space of the house by providing a link to the outdoors, while also supplying the optimal level of daylight. On the other hand, they could not detract from the efficiency of the building shell. The ENERGATE high-insulation, triple-glazed oak windows that were chosen have a thermal transmission coefficient, or U-value, of .6 W/(m²K) (watts per square meter per Kelvin), which corresponds to an R-value of 10.

From windows to rigid insulation to sealants, a range of specialized building materials that are available only in Europe make it easier and more cost-effective to build a PH there. But that situation is changing. Some European manufacturers are marketing their products here, and some American companies are producing building components that conform to PH standards. When it comes to products, building a PH in the United States is getting easier all the time.

This Brooklyn brownstone was retrofitted using the Passive House approach.

Another impediment to PH construction in the United States used to be lack of expertise, but that situation also has changed. Since the founding of PHIUS, Klingenberg and Kernagis have been working tirelessly to introduce the PH approach to an American audience. They have convened national PH conferences annually, and in 2008, PHIUS introduced a training program for PH consultants. In this program, building industry professionals are taught the principles of PH design; how to use the PHPP; climate-appropriate strategies, materials, and mechanical systems; and quality assurance.

This book chronicles the projects conceived and built by some of the earliest graduates of the PH consultant trainings. These consultants have tackled a range of challenges, from very difficult climates to retrofit constraints to lack of appropriate materials. In spite of these challenges, the projects that have been built so far in the United States represent a diversity of building types and styles. Ranch houses, brownstones, low-income housing, apartment buildings—all of these and more have been constructed to meet the PH standard in climates that range from hot and humid to extremely cold. What these examples clearly demonstrate is that buildings can use very little energy to operate and still be comfortable and beautiful—and can do so in a wide range of climates. It takes skill, creativity, and often persistence to create a PH. But once you understand that it is feasible to build a much more comfortable and much more efficient home, one that will be durable and will help to reduce carbon emissions—in short, one that will leave a positive legacy for our children—then, as Stephan Tanner says, why wouldn't you?

For more **information:**

Homes for a Changing Climate: Passive Houses in the U.S., by Katrin Klingenberg, Mike Kernagis, and Mary James, which documents the first PH projects in the United States, including the Smith House and the BioHaus, is available from Low Carbon Productions at **www.lowcarbonproductions.com**.

Extensive data on the energy performance of many of the European PHs are available at **www.cepheus.de/eng/index.html**.

CHAPTER 2

The **Steamy Side** of Passive House

Lafayette, Louisiana

Corey Saft is the owner, architect, and overall supervisor of the first Passive House to be constructed in the hot and really humid climate of southern Louisiana. A professor of architecture at the University of Louisiana at Lafayette, Saft stumbled on the PH standard after becoming frustrated with some aspects of a rival green building certification process. He was impressed enough with the performance targets of the PH standard that when the opportunity arose to build on the lot next door to his own house, he set PH certification as his goal.

It's an extremely ambitious goal, because the PH approach was originally conceived in a cold climate—where capturing and retaining the heat generated by people's daily activities is critical to its implementation. In Louisiana, heat is not usually an asset. Still, as Saft says, PH logic holds here in the steamy South; it holds, but it gets flipped. Creating a PH here is all about shedding heat, dehumidifying the air, and not giving away any coolness that has been generated in the house.

The lot next door is irregularly shaped and small—less than ⅛ acre. It's a corner lot, and even though the adjacent street is not that busy, Saft had long wanted an opportunity

to create a sanctuary, a safe space where his two young daughters could play. Putting a long, tall, thin building on the next-door lot would create that sanctuary, by blocking easy access to the street and giving shape to a sheltered courtyard between the two homes. A long, tall building would also make the most of the narrow lot's constraints. Starting with that premise, Saft pushed himself to create a home that was as efficient, and as well adapted to his site and climate, as he could make it.

Thirty-five miles from the Gulf of Mexico, Lafayette is either humid or rainy much of the year, and has rightly earned its reputation for being one of the ten wettest cities

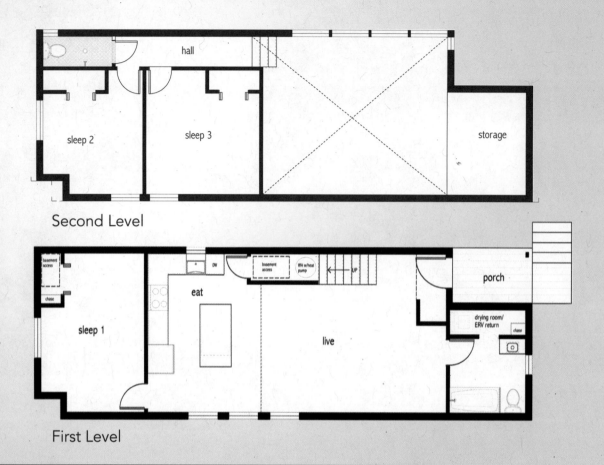

Second Level

First Level

in the United States. Its average annual rainfall is about 5 feet. The area that Saft lives in is not quite a flood zone, but it's not very far from one, either—less than two minutes by foot. Coulees, or concrete riverbeds, crisscross the city, channeling storm waters to the Vermilion River and eventually out to the Gulf.

In this climate, and particularly for this lot, tall and thin has several advantages. A thin building can make the most of cross ventilation as a cooling mechanism. A tall building maximizes the living space for the very compact 17-foot by 50-foot footprint; the interior of the house totals 1,200 square feet. The height of the building blocks the view from Saft's home of the apartments across the street. Tall

and thin also maximizes the sunlight reaching the solar panels on the new house without blocking his own home's solar access. Although the home is more modern looking than most of its neighbors, the shape actually borrows from the local architectural vernacular—the "camelback shotgun" house.

A PH doesn't just get thrown together. It's a product of thoughtful design, and that is particularly critical when you are building a home in such a challenging climate. Every feature in Saft's home contributes to the success of the structure, starting with the light-colored, metal single-pitch shed roof. The slope drains the frequent rains away from Saft's own house and toward the street,

Downstairs, three large windows that are protected by their own sun-shades open onto a small, forested glen. The prevailing breezes from the south can enter through these windows.

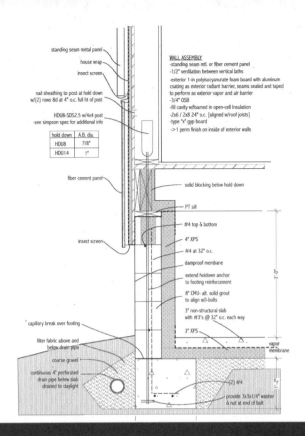

standing seam metal panel
house wrap
insect screen
nail sheathing to post at hold down
w/(2) rows 8d at 4" o.c. full ht of post
HDU8-SDS2.5 w/4x4 post
-see simpson spec for additional info

hold down	A.B. dia.
HDU8	7/8"
HDU14	1"

WALL ASSEMBLY
-standing seam mtl. or fiber cement panel
-1/2" ventilation between vertical laths
-exterior 1-in polyisocyanurate foam board with aluminum coating as exterior radiant barrier, seams sealed and taped to perform as exterior vapor and air barrier
-3/4" OSB
-fill cavity w/foamed in open-cell Insulation
-2x6 / 2x8 24" o.c. [aligned w/roof joists]
-type "x" gyp board
->1 perm finish on inside of exterior walls

fiber cement panel
insect screen

solid blocking below hold down
PT sill
#4 top & bottom
4" XPS
#4 at 32" o.c.
damproof membane
extend holdown anchor to footing reinforcement
8" CMU- alt. solid grout to align w/J-bolts
3" non-structural slab with #3's @ 32" o.c. each way
3" XPS
vapor membrane

capillary break over footing
filter fabric above and below drain pipe
coarse gravel
continuous 4" perforated drain pipe below slab drained to daylight
(2) #4
provide 3x3x1/4" washer & nut at end of bolt

3'-0"

where culverts direct it to the nearby coulee. The large overhang on the north side protects the clerestory windows just below it; on the south side the windows are placed low down on the walls and are protected by their own sunshades. The roof pitch and window placement combine to channel the prevailing winds to maximize natural ventilation through the house. The prevailing breezes from the south enter through the lower windows, while the air moving over the roof creates a force that sucks the air out of the house through its high north-facing windows, essentially producing a powerful stack effect.

Inside, Saft designed the home to give it a feeing of spaciousness and flow in spite of its small footprint. Cathedral ceilings in the double-height living room and the two upstairs bedrooms add airiness to the otherwise compact three-bedroom home. As you walk in the front door, your first view is of three large windows grouped together in the kitchen. Beyond them, a little forested glen beside a coulee beckons.

To lessen the impact of Lafayette's periodic deluges, a house in this neighborhood is traditionally raised up to 4 feet above ground level, perched over a ventilated crawl space. It was a tradition worth keeping, Saft thought—worth improving upon, in fact. PH design calls for a continuous airtight barrier, an approach that is inconsistent with a ventilated crawl space. So Saft's house sits the usual 4 feet off the ground, but over an insulated nonstructural slab-on-grade and a sealed crawl space—essentially a short basement. To promote drainage, the 3 inches of extruded polystyrene (XPS) that separates the 3½-inch concrete slab from the ground rests on a bed of gravel. The subslab insulation has an R-value of 16.

Saft had considered not putting insulation under the house, but putting insulation wings around the perimeter of the house instead. With no insulation under the slab, the house could connect thermally to the ground and tap into the near-constant 68°F that can be found just 10 or so feet below the surface. However, he decided to follow the PH practice of insulating the house from exterior temperatures from the foundation to the roof.

The short basement was constructed with walls made of concrete masonry unit (CMU) blocks, which can take periodic wetting and drying better than most materials. To address potential windstorms or hurricanes, the home was engineered with extensive tie-downs. All four corners are held down by $^7/_8$-inch threaded rod that is cast into the grade beam and attaches well up into the stud wall. The basement walls, which are lined with 4 inches of XPS on the inside, have a total R-value of 21.

Superinsulation and airtight construction are two critical principles of the PH approach. Saft designed the foundation to achieve both goals. Grade beams support the CMU block basement walls. A membrane runs under the insulated nonstructural slab and continues under these grade beams

The home has a feeling of spaciousness in spite of its small footprint.

out to the exterior. It comes back inside on top of the grade beams, goes up the inside of the CMU wall, and goes back out on top of the wall. There it is attached to the fully taped 1-inch polyisocyanurate board insulation that wraps the house and continues the vapor barrier. This

To cut down on wood waste, Saft designed the house so that uncut studs could be used for most of the framing members.

polyiso board has an R-value of 7 per inch and contains no hydrochlorofluorocarbons (HCFCs), which are ozone-depleting compounds.

Sheathing covered in a peel-and-stick underlayment topped by 2-inch polyiso forms the air barrier layer in the roof assembly. Above the polyiso, Saft specified 1 x 4 sleepers to create a ¾-inch venting air space, under the standing-seam metal roof. More than 10 inches of Icynene fill the 2 x 12 roof rafters, delivering an R-value of 55.

While careful design is essential, close attention to detail in the execution of a design is also critical to achieving an airtightness goal. Saft gives the contractor, Jaron Young of HJ Construction, a great deal of credit for the success of this project. Without his appreciation for PH principles and building science generally, Saft doubts that they would have been able to meet the PH airtightness target of 0.6 ACH_{50}. But they did. Before the drywall was installed, they performed a blower door test, which came in at 141 cubic feet per minute at 50 pascals (CFM_{50}), or 0.55 ACH. As far as Saft knows, his is the tightest house ever tested in Louisiana.

Meticulous and economical design also shows up in the exterior walls, which feature a dual-purpose rain screen. The outermost layer, fiber cement siding, both sheds moisture and operates as a whole-house shade, keeping direct sun off the inner layers of the wall assembly. Saft chose to use fiber cement siding for its durability, cost-effectiveness, and practicality. It comes prepainted, which reduces on-site labor. The fiber cement siding is nailed to ¾-inch battens that create an air gap between the siding and the Tyvek-covered, foil-faced polyiso insulation board. This air gap provides an escape channel for any water or heat that penetrates the siding. The foil facing on the insulation board acts as a radiant barrier that reflects heat back into the air gap; the heat is then vented up and out between the battens. Any water infiltration can run down and out the bottom or be evaporated away by the air traveling up the channel. An insect screen was installed at the bottom of the channel.

Termites are a big problem in the Deep South. To prevent infestations, all the wood in the house is at least 3 feet off the ground, and all vegetation is at least 2 feet from the building. A termite shield made of galvanized steel was installed at the outer edge of the top of the foundation as a further preventive measure.

Every component of the house was carefully weighed both for its contribution to the energy efficiency of the structure and for its overall environmental impact. To use no more wood than is strictly necessary and to pack as much insulation as possible into the wall assembly, Saft designed the house using advanced framing, with studs placed 24 inches on center (OC). Half the house is a double-height space, and 2 x 8 studs are used for the walls in this half. For the single-height walls, the studs are 2 x 6s. Because he wanted to reduce the use of petroleum-derived products in the structure, as well as in the operation, of the home, Saft chose to fill the wall cavities with Icynene spray foam insulation, in which castor oil replaces part of the petroleum-based polyol, and which is 100% water blown. The 2 x 6 walls have a total R-value of 28, while the 2 x 8 walls achieve an R-33.

Creating a PH here is all about **shedding heat, dehumidifying the air, and not giving away any coolness that has been generated** in the house.

With an eye to further reducing wood waste, Saft designed the house so that uncut studs could be used for most of the framing members. The wall supporting the lower end of the roof was designed to use uncut 16-foot studs, and the wall supporting the upper end of the roof used uncut 20-foot studs.

For the windows, Saft picked the SeriousWindows 501 series, with vinyl frames. The fixed windows have a U-factor of .18; the glass has a solar heat gain coefficient (SHGC) of .24. Getting glass that has this low an SHGC is particularly critical for heat management in a home that is located this far south, and that gets such a steady dose of sunlight.

The short basement houses the plumbing and the energy recovery ventilator (ERV) system; it also provides some extra storage space. The ERV is 95% efficient, according to the manufacturer, UltimateAir. In addition to ventilating and transferring heat, an ERV can dehumidify the incoming air. When the air is especially hot and humid, though, the ERV will not be able to condition the air enough to keep the house comfortable. For those days, Saft installed a Samsung 19-SEER (seasonal energy efficiency ratio) ductless mini-split heat pump—a small, two-component air-conditioning system that cools, dehumidifies, and can also heat.

As is required to achieve certification as a PH, Saft had the home modeled using the PHPP software. The software predicted that the annual electrical energy use for this home could be offset by a 3.24 kW thin-film photovoltaic (PV) system, which Saft decided to install on the roof. Preliminary results suggest that the calculation will be accurate. In the first month after the new tenants moved in, the PV system had produced more electricity than they had used.

Thanks to such careful planning, and great teamwork, the construction costs for this southern PH came in at $110/ft^2, just above Saft's goal of $100/ft^2. Meeting the PH performance targets in such a humid climate is a remarkable achievement and an excellent model—one that deserves to be copied many times over.

PASSIVE HOUSE
Verification Summary

Builder	Jaron Young, HJ Construction
PH Consultant	PHIUS
Architect	Corey Saft
City	Lafayette, Louisiana
Year	2010

Specific Space Heat Demand	9 kWh/m²/yr (0.8 kWh/ft²/yr)
Pressurization Test Result	0.55 ACH$_{50}$
Specific Primary Energy Demand (DHW, Heating, Cooling, Auxiliary, and Household Electricity)	117 kWh/m²/yr (10.8 kWh/ft²/yr)
Specific Useful Cooling Energy Demand	15 kWh/m²/yr (1.4 kWh/ft²/yr)

CHAPTER 3

A Home for
Their Future

Salem, Oregon

Sarah Evans and Stuart Rue loved their neighborhood of mostly 1920s-era homes in Salem, the capital of Oregon. It was very close to downtown—close enough that each of them could bicycle to and from work. Their own 1920s home was also special, but special in the way of a slightly annoying, still treasured older relative. It was drafty and uncomfortable, but charming. A nearby corner lot that had been empty since they moved into the neighborhood four years ago lured them into dreaming of a greener, more-comfortable home—even though they weren't really sure what a greener home would entail or whether they could afford to build one.

They read about Oregon's first Leadership in Energy and Environmental Design (LEED) Platinum house and decided to give the builders, Larry and Blake Bilyeu, a call. What they didn't know was that Blake had recently trained to become a Passive House consultant. Once he explained that with the PH approach, they could build a very comfortable, highly energy-efficient home, and build it at a price they could afford, they knew they had found the greener home they wanted. A home for their future—one that would minimize their carbon footprint, and one that fit their

budget. As Evans says, "with the PH approach, we were able to do way more than we ever dreamed we could."

The corner lot has terrific southern exposure. At first, this had Evans and Rue dreaming of all the renewable energy they could generate on their rooftop. Conversations with Blake Bilyeu reframed their dreams, turning them toward investing instead in better-insulated walls and other passive shell measures and maximizing interior solar gain. Eventually those conversations led Bilyeu to approach the Oregon Department of Energy to ask for rebates for those shell measures—rebates that would be equivalent to those

given for installing PVs. Bilyeu was successful...
but that's getting ahead of the story.

All PHs are designed for the best possible
performance in the climate where the house
is constructed. Since this 1,885 ft² home was
being built in Salem, the wall, roof, and floor
assemblies were optimized for a mixed-humid,
marine climate. Centrally located plumbing and
mechanical systems contribute to the home's
overall efficiency. But the best design can
still be defeated by poor execution, so the
Bilyeus, whenever possible, specified building
elements that would be familiar to the
subcontractors they generally worked with.
Then they tweaked those elements to achieve
the ultimate performance.

The construction of the exterior walls uses
very familiar elements, but gives them a twist.
Two 2 x 4 stud walls, separated by a 3-inch
space, form a 10½-inch-thick sandwich. Both
walls are framed 24 inches OC, but are offset
from one another by 12 inches for optimized
assembly layouts. The outer 2 x 4 wall supports
the roof load, while the inner 2 x 4 wall supports
the second-story floor system. In Salem this
double-wall design permits the use of advanced
framing for the 2 x 4 walls, with single top
plates, since each wall carries only one type of
load, and all loads are stacked in parallel paths.
This design also allowed Bilyeu to construct
walls with no thermal bridges, since the second-
story floor system does not penetrate through
to the outer wall, but bears on the inner wall
only. To decrease the amount of wood in the
walls and increase the percentage of insulation,
Bilyeu made sure to eliminate all unnecessary
trimmers and headers.

The exterior sheathing, which is ½-inch
plywood, forms the primary air barrier. It is
carefully detailed at the seams with 3M's new 8067 All
Weather Tape, which has performed exceedingly well,
according to Bilyeu. Plumbing, electrical, and ventilation
penetrations are all sealed with site-fabricated synthetic-
rubber gaskets. This wall air barrier layer ties directly to
a plywood subroof ceiling air barrier and to the floor air

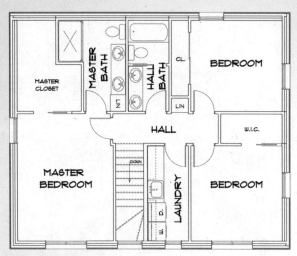

Second Level

First Level

barrier as well. At each of these intersections, the plywood
layer was thoroughly sealed to the ceiling and floor layers,
using a combination of high-performance tape and gaskets.
Windows and doors seal back to the primary air barrier
with Vycor tape.

Inside the walls, 10 inches of all-borate dense-packed
cellulose, which is made from 85% recycled paper, fill each

cavity. On the exterior, the framed walls are covered with 2 inches of expanded polystyrene (EPS) foam, over which are layered a weather-resistant barrier, wood battens, and fiber cement lap siding. The battens are on a 12-inch layout, screwed on through the foam at 24 inches OC; these battens hold up the siding. The R-value of the whole exterior wall assembly is 45.

The wall assembly was designed to dry to either side. The battens help form a ¾-inch ventilated rain screen system, designed to keep rainwater off the wall assembly and create an air space to promote the drying of any moisture that does manage to gain access. The interior of the wall is covered with latex paint—a vapor retarder, but not a barrier—to maintain the possibility of drying to the interior.

The roof system is composed of 60% postconsumer recycled metal roofing supported by premanufactured raised-heel trusses that bear only on the outer 2 x 4 wall system. The exterior wall air barrier layer joins a plywood shelf affixed to the top of the double-stud walls. The trusses rest on this shelf, which extends 2 inches into the interior; the plywood air barrier on the underside of the bottom truss chord ties in to the wall system air barrier. Below the plywood layer, 2 x 4 furring strips, 24 inches OC and on edge, run perpendicular to the truss chords and create a

wiring chase that does not penetrate the air barrier and is insulated with dense-packed cellulose. The ventilated attic is insulated with 24 inches of loose-fill cellulose, blown in. The attic access is located on the gable end of the house, to avoid penetrating the air barrier.

Ventilated crawl spaces are common in the Northwest, but building scientists have long debated their merits, and how best to modify them to improve a home's performance. For this home, Bilyeu opted to construct a floor system based on the consensus reached following an animated discussion between an East Coast building science expert and Washington State University's energy program researchers on best practices for the Pacific Northwest climate. The resulting sealed floor system over a ventilated crawl space combines the best PH practices of a well-sealed envelope with the local practice of ventilating a crawl space to provide an exit pathway for moisture. In this system, the airtight component is the $1^{1}/_{8}$-inch plywood subfloor, with all seams sealed with All Weather Tape. I joists, placed 24 inches OC and insulated with dense-packed cellulose, support the subfloor. The joists do not extend to the exterior; they terminate at an interior rim that is separated from the exterior rim by 3 inches of XPS foam. The underside of the floor joists is covered with 1½ inches of EPS foam, with the joints and all penetrations sealed.

All of the windows are Serious Windows fiberglass-framed 725 series, but with different glazing, depending on the orientation. For the south-facing façade Bilyeu chose High SHGC glazing with HM-88 film, clear glass, and krypton fill. This glazing has a U-value of .178 and an SHGC of .563. For the other three façades he used the Low SHGC glazing with SC-75 film, Cardinal 272 glass, and krypton fill. Although PH-related research has shown that windows installed in the center of a wall assembly deliver the best thermal performance, Bilyeu specified installing the windows where he customarily installs them—on the exterior side of the wall assembly in parallel with the EPS. This installation, and the required flashing details, are familiar to his construction crew—an advantage that Bilyeu felt outweighed the small loss in thermal performance, given the relatively mild climate in Salem.

All unnecessary trimmers and headers were eliminated to decrease the amount of wood in the walls and increase the percentage of insulation.

Thanks to a design guided by the PH approach and PHPP modeling, internal and solar heat gains will recoup over 60% of the home's annual heat loss.

The doors presented a bit of a puzzle for Bilyeu. The clients wanted doors that would allow them to meet the PH performance targets. That was the relatively easy part. Bilyeu installed three Therma-Tru wood edge insulated fiberglass units with upgraded gasketing, a five-point lock system, and a U-value of .13. The hard part was the dog. How could their faithful companion come and go through one of those energy-efficient doors when he needed to roam? Adopting a never-say-never attitude, Bilyeu searched for and found the extremely well-sealed Freedom Pet Pass pet door, which he installed in the Therma-Tru back door, so the dog could get in and out of the mudroom.

This Freedom Pet Pass door made everyone happy, especially Bilyeu, when a subsequent blower door test came in at 0.2 ACH_{50}—well below the 0.6 ACH performance target. Bilyeu's team performed the blower door test as soon as the windows, doors, and pet door were installed—long before insulation and drywall could block access to any potentially leaky areas. Bilyeu attributes this outstanding airtightness level in no small part to the care that his subcontractors took to create and maintain an intact air barrier layer. The Bilyeus have been working with most of these subcontractors for several years building

high-performance homes, and their education has kept pace with the Bilyeus' growing expertise in advanced building techniques.

To supply fresh air, Bilyeu chose a Sterling UltimateAir RecoupAerator 200dx ERV, with returns in the two bathrooms, powder room, kitchen, and laundry room, and supplies in the bedrooms and living areas. Transfer grilles were installed as needed, to allow air to seep into or out of a closed room and to adjust any pressure imbalances. Timers in the bathrooms boost the ventilation speed to quickly exhaust humidity or odors. In the kitchen, a recirculating charcoal filter range hood collects and filters out cooking grease, so that it can't get sucked into the ventilation system and damage the core of the ERV. The clients selected a Bosch condenser clothes dryer, which condenses moisture out of the clothes rather than blowing hot air over them, and which needs no exhaust vent. The condensed moisture drains out the bottom of the unit.

Thanks to a design guided by the PH approach and PHPP modeling, internal and solar heat gains recoup over 60% of the home's annual heat loss. Further heating will be supplied by a Fujitsu 26-SEER 9,000 Btu per hour (Btu/h) wall-mounted mini-split heat pump in the main living area.

Bilyeu specified installing the windows where he customarily installs them—on the exterior side of the wall assembly in parallel with the EPS.

This was the smallest, most efficient unit that Bilyeu could find. In order to meet local code requirements, he put small electric-resistance heaters in the other rooms.

Evans and Rue don't expect to use the supplementary heaters very often, and they intend to watch all of their electrical consumption closely. A countertop graphical user interface that displays the moment-to-moment electrical usage in the house will make it easy to do that. This immediate feedback will help Evans and Rue to understand and control their energy consumption.

To minimize the energy requirements for water heating, Evans and Rue chose a Mazdon Thermomax 40-tube evacuated solar-thermal system tied to a 120-gallon Ruud Solar Servant tank that incorporates an electric heating element for backup. In addition, the plumbing drains in the upstairs bathroom feed a 7-foot-long, 3-inch-diameter wastewater gravity film exchange system that scavenges heat from the shower drain water and preheats the incoming cold water.

Low-flow, high-efficiency showerheads were used at all showers to reduce both heating energy and water use. Other water conservation devices include dual-flush toilets in all bathrooms, and 1½ gallon per minute (gpm) aerators

at all faucets. The entire house is preplumbed for a future gravity-fed graywater system that would reuse sink and shower drain water for irrigation.

Although efficiency topped the list of building concerns for Evans and Rue, they also wanted to minimize the environmental impact of the materials used in the home, and to reuse and recycle any and all materials that they could. In keeping with their preferences, Bilyeu took care not to introduce toxins and products that might offgas toxins into the home during construction. All interior materials—trim work, cabinets, and underlayment—are made with no added urea formaldehyde. All paints and all other coatings, such as the sealant used on the wood floor, are either low- or no-VOC (volatile organic compound) products. The main floor features Oregon white oak flooring certified by the Forest Stewardship Council (FSC) that is locally grown and milled at the Zena Forest, just west of Salem. When the city required them to replace cracked sidewalk segments in front of their house, they reused the pieces to create the walkway to the house and permeable hardscapes in the backyard.

In addition to being certified as a Passive House, this home is the first in the state to meet the Oregon

"Since moving in, we've only turned on the heat once briefly, and **everything has remained a nice, even temperature. I love it!**"

Department of Energy's High Performance Home standard with renewable equivalent shell measures. Builders of homes that meet this standard's criteria can receive rebates for the energy savings that their very well-insulated wall and roof assemblies will create, in much the same way that builders who install renewable-energy measures are eligible for rebates. This home is also the first to meet the Energy Trust of Oregon's Advanced Performance Home requirements. Finally, it is third-party certified to meet both the Earth Advantage Platinum and Energy Star home standards.

Building to the PH standard came at a price, but it was a pretty competitive price. Bilyeu compared the cost of this PH construction to the average cost of the last three custom homes his company had built. The Passive House cost about $18,000—or roughly 6%—more. Labor to build the double walls, rather than the company's usual wall assembly, cost an additional $3,000, and Bilyeu paid an extra $4,000 to buy more insulation than he would use for the typical custom house. There were increased costs for other materials as well, but nothing astronomical. Even the much better-performing Serious windows didn't cost much more than the aluminum-clad wood windows that Bilyeu was used to installing.

Much of this cost increase was offset by rebates. A tax credit from the Oregon Department of Energy netted Bilyeu's company $8,440, and it received another $4,000 from the Energy Trust of Oregon for meeting the trust's Advanced Performance Home requirements. After the rebates, the PH cost only about $6,500 more.

Did the cost increase translate into noticeably better performance? In a word, yes, although it is much too soon to talk about annual energy use. In the late spring of 2010, just after Bilyeu finished the home, he walked around inside with his digital infrared (IR) thermometer in his hand. The heat hadn't been on in the house for weeks, yet in every room the temperature was the same. In the far corner of the upstairs closet, it was 68°F; in the far corner of the downstairs office, 68°F. Everywhere he went, 68°F. Even though he knew the house should perform this way, Bilyeu said, it was very exciting to get this confirmation. Evans and Rue are thrilled. As Evans said a couple of weeks later, "Since moving in, we've only turned on the heat once briefly, and everything has remained a nice, even temperature. I love it!"

PASSIVE HOUSE
Verification Summary

Builder	Larry and Blake Bilyeu
PH Consultant	Blake Bilyeu
Architect	Larry and Blake Bilyeu
City	Salem, Oregon
Year	2009

Specific Space Heat Demand	4.02 kBtu/ft²/yr (1.2 kWh/ft²/yr)
Pressurization Test Result	0.2 ACH$_{50}$
Specific Primary Energy Demand (DHW, Heating, Cooling, Auxiliary, and Household Electricity)	22.8 kBtu/ft²/yr (6.7 kWh/ft²/yr)
Specific Useful Cooling Energy Demand	4 kBtu/ft²/yr (1.2 kWh/ft²/yr)

CHAPTER 4

A Wine Country
Retrofit

Sonoma, California

Rick Milburn, owner of Solar Knights Construction in Napa, California, was a bit skeptical of the Passive House approach when he first heard of it. It's not that he thinks energy-efficient building techniques are unimportant; he's been concerned about the environmental implications of his industry for more than a decade. But the PH requirements seemed extreme, perhaps unrealistic. He was skeptical—and intrigued—enough that he flew out to Urbana, Illinois, for the Passive House consultant trainings.

Convinced of its efficacy, but still skeptical that this approach could be executed on a regular basis, he flew to Germany for the Passivhaus conference there. "I had to go see PH in Germany because I still didn't believe." He does now. The conference, with its exhibit hall full of products geared to help builders meet the PH standard and its tour of local PH buildings, persuaded him that this construction approach was a practical means of sharply reducing a project's carbon footprint. Soon afterward he sold an environmentally concerned client on remodeling her Sonoma home to meet PH standards.

The town of Sonoma is about as picturesque as a town can be, especially in spring, with flowers and trees in bloom everywhere you look and vine-covered, terraced hills off in the distance. It's easy to forget at this time of year that summer can mean days and weeks with temperatures in the 90s and above, while winter ushers in many nights in the 20s and many more in the 30s. It's not a harsh, unforgiving climate, but there's a reason why Sonoma's early mission buildings had thick walls with whitewashed coats.

His client's home had been built in the 1960s and consisted of two single-story structures connected by a

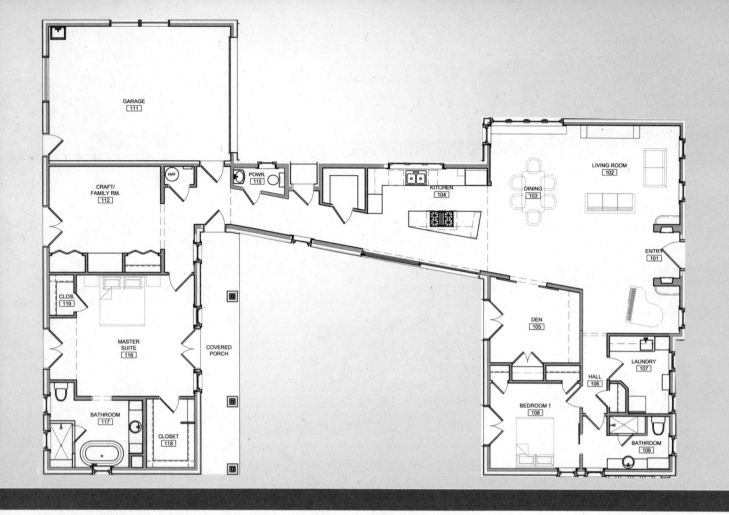

breezeway. The client wanted to turn the existing structures into one low-impact, energy-efficient home that she could retire in, that would be comfortable for her as she aged, and that wouldn't cost much to maintain. Her mother's aging and recent death had been eye opening in terms of the remodeling needed to make a home work for this stage of life. The financial crisis and the excesses of Wall Street confirmed her view that flashiness and greed need to yield to an appreciation of a longer-term horizon and a sustainable future. She chose to pursue a PH certification because this standard spoke to her sense of stewardship and building for durability. In addition, she liked the fact that PH was designed to be adapted to local climates, and she was genuinely excited about using the PH approach to create a cleaner and greener net zero home.

Postreconstruction, the two renovated structures have been integrated to form one 2,400 ft² U-shaped house that surrounds an attractively landscaped courtyard. The former breezeway has been converted into a light-filled kitchen that is dominated by an incredibly beautiful, 16-foot-wide, double-pane lift-and-slide glass door. The kitchen is the true centerpiece of this home and doubles as a hallway that connects the master suite and family room to the dining room, great room, and guest rooms.

In constructing the walls of his Sonoma PH project, Milburn used an approach first conceived in Canada, the PERSIST, or Pressure Equalized Rain Screen Insulated Structure Technique. PERSIST, which was developed by Canada's National Research Council, advocates putting the air barrier and insulation on all sides of the exterior of the building to reduce thermal bridging and keep moisture out of the structure. This technique is very closely aligned with the PH approach to construction. Milburn had read

Shading strategies include a covered 8-foot porch on the west-facing side.

about the technique a few years ago, but this was his first opportunity to implement it.

For this house, Milburn wrapped all of the structural sheathing, which consists of FSC-certified ½-inch plywood, in Grace Ice and Water Shield, a rubberized asphalt adhesive backed by a layer of high-density polyethylene, to form a continuous air barrier. In new construction, the air barrier would be continued under the slab, but in a retrofit that's not possible, so Milburn installed a layer of Stego wrap on top of the slab and taped it to the Ice and Shield using Protecto wrap tape. To keep the air barrier continuous, all mechanical, plumbing, and electrical runs are in interior walls. All penetrations through the air barrier are booted and taped to the polyethylene layer. The boot, which is also mechanically fastened to the sheathing, is filled with closed-cell foam, as are all pipes carrying electrical wires.

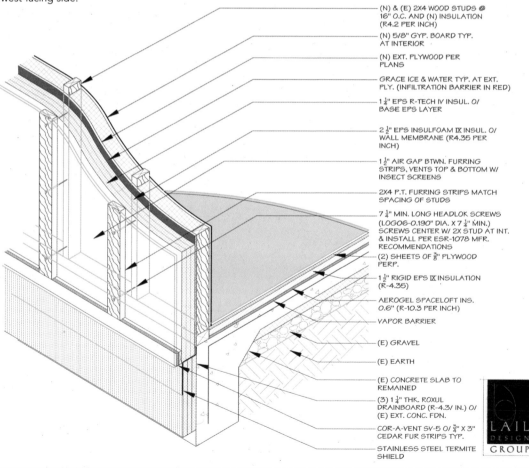

(N) & (E) 2X4 WOOD STUDS @ 16" O.C. AND (N) INSULATION (R4.2 PER INCH)

(N) 5/8" GYP. BOARD TYP. AT INTERIOR

(N) EXT. PLYWOOD PER PLANS

GRACE ICE & WATER TYP. AT EXT. PLY. (INFILTRATION BARRIER IN RED)

1¼" EPS R-TECH IV INSUL. O/ BASE EPS LAYER

2½" EPS INSULFOAM IX INSUL. O/ WALL MEMBRANE (R4.35 PER INCH)

1½" AIR GAP BTWN. FURRING STRIPS, VENTS TOP & BOTTOM W/ INSECT SCREENS

2X4 P.T. FURRING STRIPS MATCH SPACING OF STUDS

7¼" MIN. LONG HEADLOK SCREWS (LOG06-0.190" DIA. X 7¼" MIN.) SCREWS CENTER W/ 2X STUD AT INT. & INSTALL PER ESR-1078 MFR. RECOMMENDATIONS

(2) SHEETS OF ⅝" PLYWOOD PERP.

1½" RIGID EPS IX INSULATION (R-4.35)

AEROGEL SPACELOFT INS. 0.6" (R-10.3 PER INCH)

VAPOR BARRIER

(E) GRAVEL

(E) EARTH

(E) CONCRETE SLAB TO REMAINED

(3) 1¼" THK. ROXUL DRAINBOARD (R-4.3/ IN.) O/ (E) EXT. CONC. FDN.

COR-A-VENT SV-5 O/ ¾" X 3" CEDAR FUR STRIPS TYP.

STAINLESS STEEL TERMITE SHIELD

LAIL DESIGN GROUP

The kitchen is dominated by a beautiful, 16-foot wide, double pane lift-and-slide glass door.

Over the air barrier a continuous layer of EPS was added, with 3¾ inches on the walls, and 2½ inches under the roof. Milburn chose to source his EPS from Insulfoam, because this foam is made with postconsumer and postindustrial materials, and the company will take any waste back; it's a cradle-to-cradle system.

Originally, Milburn had planned to use rigid mineral wool insulation, because it is not a petroleum product, but the insulation sample he got didn't perform well enough when he tested it for compressive strength. The insulation's compressive strength was critical for this job because the siding Milburn prefers requires the construction of a rain screen that is heftier than most. Instead of using typically lightweight battens, this rain screen uses 2 x 4s nailed on over the Insulfoam. The siding, which is made by Bodyguard from FSC-certified pine wood that is grown sustainably in New Zealand, is nailed to the 2 x 4s. The beefed-up battens were needed in order to be in compliance with the siding warranty, which requires

1½-inch nail penetration into wood. Below grade, where the siding warranty isn't an issue, Milburn specified 3¾ inches of mineral wool as subgrade insulation, which he has covered with a stucco finish.

Interior walls, waterproof membrane, exterior insulation, and then cladding—those are the basic ingredients of the PERSIST layer. This retrofit includes several variations in the wall assemblies, with some walls being rebuilt from existing ones and others being built from scratch. In general, though, the exterior wall assemblies have an R-value of 31.

Since the persistent, as in almost-guaranteed-to-be-shining, summer sun can turn homes with poorly insulated roofs into baking ovens, the roof assembly boasts an R-value of 75. Fifteen inches of high-density fiberglass insulation was installed using the blown-in blanket system (BIBS) on the underside of the roof sheathing. In this system, fiberglass is blown into place behind a mesh fabric, providing for a uniform density of insulation. Milburn also

Builder Rick Milburn has educated all of his long-term subcontractors about the PH approach.

used the BIBS to install from 3½ to 5½ inches of fiberglass on the interior of the exterior walls. Formaldehyde-free R-13 batts were used on all interior walls to reduce sound transmission.

Milburn chose a light-colored, standing-seam metal roof. Metal roofs outlast most other types of roof and have a relatively high proportion of recycled content. A light color will increase the roof's reflectivity, reducing solar heat gain. Shading strategies to further reduce solar heat gain include 27-inch overhangs all around the house, except on the west-facing side, which has a covered 8-foot porch. A vine-covered trellis shields the long kitchen window.

In a retrofit, it isn't possible to insulate under the slab, so the top of the slab is the next best choice. Complicating this option was the fact that the two preexisting parts of the home had slabs at different heights, so Milburn and his team had to devise a separate insulation strategy for each of these areas. In the parts of the house where he had only a little more than 2 inches to work with, he installed

1½ inches of EPS on top of the slab, along with 0.6 inches of Spaceloft, to achieve a total R-value of 14. Spaceloft is a flexible, high-R-value-per-inch material that is well suited for applications where space is at a premium. In the front section of the house, where there was more room, he installed 4 inches of EPS on top of the slab.

All of the windows in this retrofit are new, Optiwin 3-wood, triple-pane units that have an overall R-value of 8.3. The glazing has a U-value equal to .11, or an R-value of 9. The SHGC for these windows is .53, which means that 53% of the solar heat gets transmitted through the glass. These tilt-and-turn windows have thermally broken frames and multipoint locking hardware that ensure a tight seal when the windows are closed. Milburn has been very impressed with the quality and the attention to detail that evidently went into the design and manufacture of the Optiwin windows. The installation of the first window was a bit tricky, since the installation video was narrated in German, but after the first one, all the others were installed easily and quickly.

The kitchen's lift-and-slide glass door and the wooden front door are also Optiwin products. The door to the garage has to be fire rated, so Milburn is building his own door to meet the required specifications.

Milburn's almost obsessive air barrier strategy and his construction crew's thorough execution paid off, as the house easily met the PH airtightness performance requirement—a remarkable achievement for a retrofit. A first blower door test, conducted before the siding had been installed, came in at an inspiring 0.4 ACH_{50}. The house achieved this level even though, as Milburn noticed after the test, one conduit had yet to be thoroughly sealed. The final blower door test was even more impressive— 0.31 ACH_{50}.

While insulating to retain heat is critical in constructing a PH, almost as important is supplying fresh air that is warmed by recycled heat from the outgoing stale air. To do this job, Milburn installed an UltimateAir RecoupAerator ERV in the centrally located pantry. Exhaust ducts in the bathrooms and kitchen pull odors and moisture from those rooms. Transfer grilles were installed over all interior doors to ensure a properly balanced airflow in the house.

The ERV has a rated heat recovery efficiency of 95% at full flow. Heat is supplied to the unit by a water-to-air heat

Milburn's subcontractors are enthusiastic about the PH approach and excited to be creating **truly efficient and durable homes**.

exchanger. The water is preheated by a solar-thermal system mounted on the roof. The solar-heated water is stored in an 80-gallon solar-thermal storage tank. If the temperature in the tank drops below 110°F, a Rinnai on-demand, direct-vent gas water heater kicks into gear and boosts the water's temperature to 120°F. For more-extreme weather conditions, there is a backup mini-split heat pump, with an output capacity of 12,000 Btu. While this heat pump will rarely be needed in winter, it may get called into service in summer to cool the incoming air.

The old house had a conventional fireplace and chimney, but that was removed to eliminate a major source of air leakage. The chimney was structurally unsound anyway. To provide that nostalgic connection to fire, the client chose to install an EcoSmart ventless fireplace that burns ethanol. The combustion by-products of this fuel source are carbon dioxide (CO_2), steam, and heat, which is why no direct venting to the outdoors is required.

The only other combustion appliance in the house is a gas cooktop, which has a recirculation hood, complete with charcoal filter, mounted just above it to capture grease and cooking odors. A return grille 6 feet from the stove draws any remaining cooking by-products out of the kitchen and into the ventilation system. The clothes dryer is an electrical condensing dryer, which needs no exhaust to the outside. Moisture from the wet clothes collects in a trap that is emptied periodically. To ensure the overall electrical efficiency of the house, the client opted to use no incandescent lighting. All of the bulbs are either compact fluorescents (CFLs) or light-emitting diodes (LEDs).

In Sonoma, which suffers intermittently from drought, water efficiency is almost as important as energy efficiency. That beautiful landscaping—it's watered by the rain collected in the newly installed 10,000-gallon underground rain catchment system, manufactured by Cudo. That tank should supply one-third of the house's landscaping needs. Finding subcontractors who are willing to put in the extra effort required to meet the PH standard can be difficult in some places, but this has not been a problem for Milburn. He has worked with the subcontractors he employs for many years, and has educated them along the way. As his understanding and appreciation of how to construct more-efficient buildings has evolved, so has theirs. According to Milburn, they are enthusiastic about the PH approach and excited to be creating truly efficient and durable homes.

As for Milburn, his appreciation of the PH standard and its practicality has also grown during this retrofit. He calculates that the extra materials and labor needed to meet the PH standard probably cost about 15% more than a conventional retrofit would have cost. With the projected energy savings, those extra costs should be paid back in nine years, or about as long as the payback period for installing PV. The experience he gained from this project will make it that much easier to meet the PH standard on his next project. In fact, according to Milburn, building to meet the PH standard in this part of California is very straightforward—it's what every builder can and should do.

PASSIVE HOUSE
Verification Summary

Builder	Rick Milburn, Solar Knights Construction	Specific Space Heat Demand	1.24 kWh/ft²/yr
PH Consultant	Graham Irwin	Pressurization Test Result	.31ACH₅₀
Architect	Jarrod Denton, Lail Design	Specific Primary Energy Demand (DHW, Heating, Cooling, Auxiliary, and Household Electricity)	8.12 kWh/ft²/yr
City	Sonoma, California	Specific Useful Cooling Energy Demand	0.36 kWh/ft²/yr
Year	2010		

CHAPTER 5

PH in the **High Desert**: The Breezeway House

Salt Lake City, Utah

Long before he became an architect, Dave Brach of Brach Design in Salt Lake City, Utah, had been drawn to the concept of sustainability. The idea of doing only what the earth could sustain seemed entirely reasonable to him, even as a college student. When he became a licensed architect and started his own practice, he searched for a design tool that would allow him to make his projects sustainable from an energy consumption standpoint. Nothing fit the bill—until he read a short article about Passive Houses in late 2007.

In May 2008 he participated in the first PH consultant training. The PHPP modeling software was what he had been seeking: a tool that allowed him to design for low energy consumption in a quantifiable way.

That spring he had started planning a home for clients who had approached him because they wanted a house with a clean, modern look. Efficiency was not at the top of their list of requirements, but they weren't indifferent to efficiency, either. As Brach progressed through the training, and reported back to them about what he had learned, they became progressively more excited about the PH concept. Cost was a consideration, so he did some financial analyses comparing the combined up-front construction costs and likely operating costs of a conventional home with those of a PH. He estimated that a PH would run $8 to $10 more per square foot to build than a conventional home. Operating cost savings would be about $950 on an annual basis, and would increase as energy prices rose. The results won his clients over; they decided that their new home would be a PH.

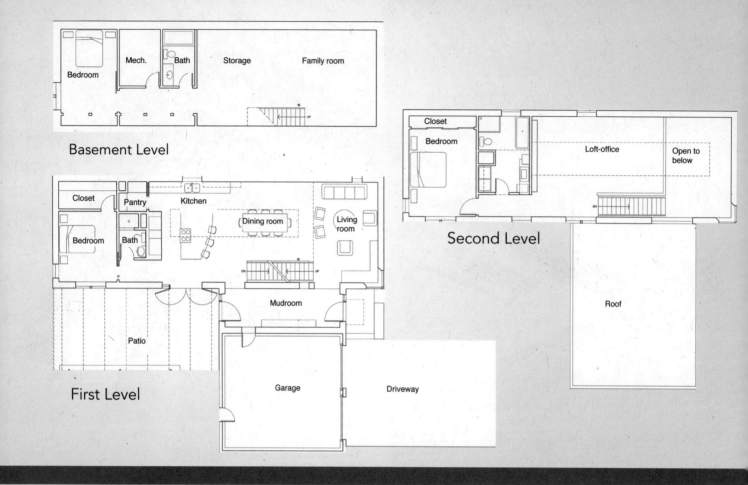

Basement Level

First Level

Second Level

Salt Lake City is high desert country, cold and often snowy in winter, and really hot and dry in summer. In winter, snow showers and sunny days trade off, so warming a house with passive-solar heat isn't as challenging as it might be. Cooling passively is another story. In summer, cloudless skies bring very hot days and nights that cool as the sun dips; a 30°F temperature swing in one day is simply average. In this desert climate, shading and night flushing are critical cooling tactics, as is the use of thermal mass to absorb heat during the day and to release it at night, when cooler temperatures prevail.

Although passive-solar heating in winter isn't that difficult, it does require adequate glazing area on the south façade, which poses a challenge for some sites, especially this one. The clients' lot is on a street that runs north and south, so Brach had to orient the home on an east-west axis. The clients wanted a two-car garage and a short driveway. Long driveways may have visual appeal, but in snow country they just mean more shoveling. A large maple tree that the clients wanted to keep graced the northeast corner of the yard, which meant no driveway on the north side. And a local zoning ordinance requires attached garages in side lots. Altogether, these constraints meant that Brach had to put an attached garage on the south side of the house. As he says, that was tough. His solution was to minimize and soften the look of the garage by installing two small garage doors, instead of one large one, and cladding the structure in wood. He also created a light-filled, enclosed walkway that connects the garage to the 3,700 ft² house. This entry structure is flanked by glass doors that lead to the front and back yards, respectively,

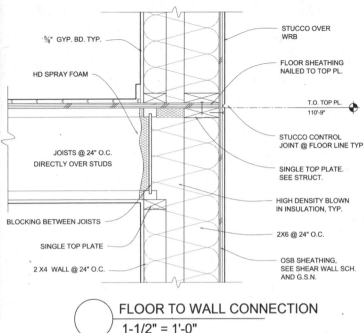

5⁄8" GYP. BD. TYP.

HD SPRAY FOAM

JOISTS @ 24" O.C.
DIRECTLY OVER STUDS

BLOCKING BETWEEN JOISTS

SINGLE TOP PLATE

2 X4 WALL @ 24" O.C.

STUCCO OVER
WRB

FLOOR SHEATHING
NAILED TO TOP PL.

T.O. TOP PL.
110'-9"

STUCCO CONTROL
JOINT @ FLOOR LINE TYP.

SINGLE TOP PLATE.
SEE STRUCT.

HIGH DENSITY BLOWN
IN INSULATION, TYP.

2X6 @ 24" O.C.

OSB SHEATHING,
SEE SHEAR WALL SCH.
AND G.S.N.

FLOOR TO WALL CONNECTION
1-1/2" = 1'-0"

The wood-clad, enclosed breezeway between the garage and the house softens the look of the building and permits easy access to the front and back yards.

giving it the feeling of an open breezeway. That's the inspiration for this home's moniker, the Breezeway House.

After orientation, glazing and shading are the two factors that most influence solar gain. To maximize solar access in winter, Brach designed the house with smaller east- and west-facing façades than the south-facing one, and increased the glazing area on the south side. All of the windows are from Serious Windows and feature fiberglass frames with double-pane glazing plus a suspended low-emissivity (low-e) film between the two panes of glass. The units on the south façade have an SHGC of .51. Those on the east, west, and north façades, have an SHGC of .31. The overall U-value of the windows is .18.

To shield the interior from the desert sun in summer, all the south-facing windows have custom-designed 18-inch shade awnings, made from cedar to match the garage. Brach scaled back the size of the awning for one window on the southeast corner of the house, because it has a grand view of Mt. Olympus, one of the handsomest mountains in the Wasatch Range, according to Brach. Behind the house is a less-monumental, but still very handsome, feature—a patio surrounded by a 30-foot by 20-foot boxlike steel structure that creates the feeling of an outdoor room. A fabric awning strung on steel cables that run from the house to the patio shades this outdoor living space, along with the west-facing glass patio door and the ground floor windows at the back of the house.

To absorb and ameliorate the daily temperature swings, Brach installed a 4-inch-thick concrete floor in the basement and a 2-inch-thick concrete floor on the first floor. Concrete countertops in the bathroom and kitchen provide even more thermal mass. Since the PH approach was not conceived in desert country, thermal mass is not emphasized in PH training, so Brach did not rely on the use of thermal mass as much as he now thinks he could have. In future desert PHs, Brach will look for opportunities to incorporate even more mass into his designs.

To absorb the daily temperature swings that are typical in this desert climate, Brach specified concrete floors in the basement and on the first floor.

To insulate the house from the ground, Brach is using 8 inches of EPS laid under the basement's concrete floor. Under the EPS is a polyethylene vapor barrier, and under that, a 4-inch layer of gravel provides drainage. The basement, which is fully conditioned, houses a bedroom and a family room.

All of the exterior walls in the house are constructed using a double-wall assembly—one inner wall and one outer wall. In the basement, the inner walls are conventional 2 x 4 stud walls, insulated with high-density blown-in fiberglass. The outer walls are built with 13½-inch-thick insulating concrete forms (ICFs). The ICFs form a foam-and-concrete sandwich, with 8 inches of concrete in the middle and 2¾ inches of foam on either side. The R-value of the total wall assembly is 36.

Above grade, the exterior double-wall assembly consists of two stud walls—a 2 x 4 inner wall and a 2 x 6 outer wall, both 24 inches OC, with a single top plate and a single bottom plate. The exterior finish is a fairly conventional ½-inch Portland cement-based stucco. Both of these wall cavities are insulated with high-density blown-in fiberglass, giving the overall wall assembly an R-value of 44.

The double-wall assembly permits the various loads in the house to be supported by different walls. The stud wall in the basement carries the first-floor load, while the outer ICF wall carries the second floor and roof. On the first floor, the outer stud wall carries the roof load, while the inner stud wall carries the second-floor load.

To create a continuous air barrier, the integral components of the wall assemblies were carefully sealed, with particular attention to all joints. In the basement, the concrete of the ICF provides an airtight layer. An EPDM (ethylene propylene diene monomer) gasket at the sill plate forms an airtight connection between the basement walls and the above-grade ones. The first- and second-floor walls are sheathed with oriented strand board (OSB), which was thoroughly sealed with caulk and glue, to form the airtight layer. The air barrier is continued up to the top of the house with a carefully sealed OSB ceiling under the roof joists.

Passive-solar and internal heat gains from such activities as cooking, cleaning, and showering will supply about 70% of the owner's heating needs.

Brach worked closely with the general contractor to ensure that the air barrier would be installed correctly. Indeed, Brach took a very hands-on approach, working as a member of the framing crew for the first three months. As soon as the house was framed up, with all of the sheathing on and caulked, and with the windows installed, the first blower door test was conducted. The result was much more than satisfactory—0.6 ACH_{50}—which meant that the Breezeway House already met the PH performance target. But Brach didn't rest on his laurels. He specified careful sealing of the interior drywall, and thorough caulking where it met the bottom and top plates, so the drywall could act as a secondary air barrier and also keep interior moisture out of the wall assembly. Throughout the house he had airtight electrical boxes installed, to prevent leakage around those penetrations. A final blower door test proved how successful these strategies—and their implementation—were, coming in at just 0.46 ACH_{50}.

Homes this tight require mechanical ventilation, which can also serve to deliver heat in the winter. To serve this dual purpose, Brach chose an Ultimate Air RecoupAerator ERV, with a hot water coil installed in line with the fresh-air intake. A 900-foot-long polyethylene ground loop, installed 6 feet below finish grade, passively warms the incoming ventilation air. A solar-thermal system heats a glycol solution that then warms the in-line coil, assisted by an electric-resistance backup heater, when necessary. This system also supplies the domestic hot water (DHW).

According to Brach's PHPP modeling, passive-solar and internal heat gains from the residents' activities will provide about 70% of the owners' heating needs. The solar-thermal panels will meet about 80% of the DHW demand and about 15% of the space heat demand over the course of the winter. For the coldest hours of the winter, when the demand for heat will exceed the ERV's ability to deliver it, Brach installed a supplemental means of delivering heat—radiant tubing in the basement slab and entry slab. Since peak heat load conditions will prevail during only about 2% of the winter hours, he expects that this supply will rarely be needed.

Having completed one PH, Brach looks forward to experimenting with different architectural approaches to create other homes that are **highly energy efficient and truly sustainable**.

The passive cooling measures that Brach designed for this house greatly reduce its cooling load, but they can't cut it to zero. Fortunately for the homeowners, the hot, dry desert climate is a perfect environment for an extremely efficient air conditioner—an evaporative cooler—to handle the remaining load. Evaporative coolers have been used in one form or another for decades in desert climates; in its most basic form, a cooler is a fan blowing air over a wet surface, such as a pad. The basic evaporative cooler adds moist, cool air to a house, which can be pleasant but can also create indoor humidity problems. Brach installed a more-advanced OASys two-stage or indirect/direct evaporative cooler, which doesn't add as much moisture to the home as do traditional coolers. The first stage of the two-stage cooler uses a heat exchanger to cool the incoming air without adding moisture; the second stage uses a fan to blow this precooled air over a more-traditional wet medium. The small amount of water used to wet the medium is automatically purged periodically. The cooler is ducted separately from the ventilation system, and can be used in a nighttime cooling mode to pull outside air in and flush the house when the outdoor temperature falls below 75°F. According to OASys, this system produces up to 3½ tons of cooling while using less than 600 watts, delivering the equivalent of better than 40 SEER.

PH certification does not require homeowners to offset their electrical demand with electricity generated by PV, nor does it even credit them for doing so, but these homeowners chose to install a 2.2 kW solar-electric system. The PV panels will generate electricity in the summer and send it back to the grid, essentially banking the excess to compensate for the increased demand in winter, when most of the electricity used will go toward meeting the heat demand.

Calculating the additional cost of getting a house to meet the PH standard isn't straightforward. A custom home is always a one-of-a-kind project, making direct comparisons difficult. That said, Brach has calculated the increased cost of the Breezeway to be roughly 8% over that of a similar custom home that met code in Salt Lake City. The homeowners are more than satisfied with the high-quality, highly efficient home they now live in, and think the extra expense was well justified.

Having completed one PH, Brach looks forward to experimenting with different architectural approaches to create other homes that are highly energy efficient and truly sustainable. His goal for his next PH in a desert climate is to lower both the cooling load and the heating load to the point where both needs could be met with one air-to-air split-system heat pump. Brach estimates that the total installed cost of the heating-and-cooling system for an average-sized home would be just $8,000. Meeting this goal would make PH more affordable for more people—creating a more-sustainable built environment overall.

PASSIVE HOUSE
Verification Summary

Builder	Fisher Custom Building
PH Consultant	Brach Design LLC
Architect	Brach Design LLC
City	Salt Lake City, Utah
Year	2009

Specific Space Heat Demand	13 kWh/m²/yr (1.2 kWh/ft²/yr)
Pressurization Test Result	0.5 ACH$_{50}$
Specific Primary Energy Demand (DHW, Heating, Cooling, Auxiliary, and Household Electricity)	98 kWh/m²/yr (9.1 kWh/ft²/yr)
Specific Useful Cooling Energy Demand	1 kWh/m²/yr (0.1 kWh/ft²/yr)

CHAPTER 6

The Passive House in the Woods

The Town of Hudson, Wisconsin

On a cold winter day—and there really aren't many other kinds of winter day in The Town of Hudson, Wisconsin—it's obvious why the heating energy that a home uses would be a homeowner's prime concern. Winter temperatures can and do stay below 30°F for weeks, even months, at a time. A Passive House is a natural fit for this climate—in theory—but in reality very few PHs have been built to withstand such a cold climate.

In 2009 a concerned homeowner decided to take on this challenge, and the result was the Passive House in the Woods, the first PH built in Wisconsin.

The homeowner started researching very efficient and very healthy homes when his wife was diagnosed with cancer. He came upon an article about PHs and then, delving deeper into the subject, read *Homes for a Changing Climate*. As he says, he knew as soon as he read the book that he had found the house he wanted. The book's directory listings led him to Tim Eian, a certified Passive

House consultant, who helped him assemble the team that would transform a concept into a sustainably built, easy-to-maintain, healthy, efficient home.

The 1,900 ft² two-story home was dubbed the Passive House in the Woods because it sits on a scenic, roughly 1-acre lot that borders undeveloped, heavily wooded land. The property overlooks the St. Croix River valley and provides stunning views, as well as prime passive-solar exposure. Eian sited and designed the house to work with the natural landscape and minimize its impact on the

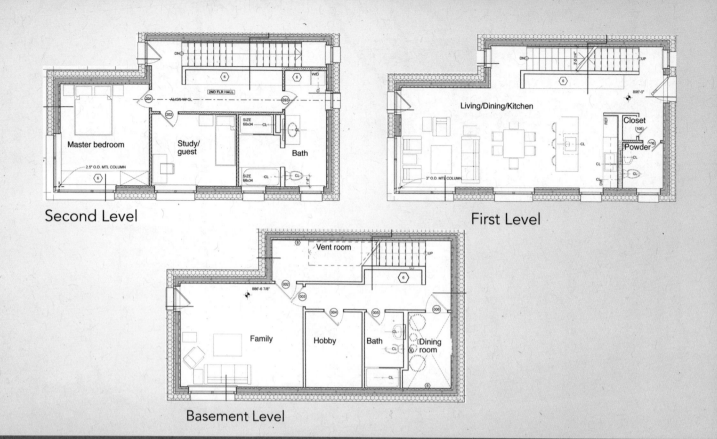

Second Level

First Level

Basement Level

wooded character of the lot. A landscape architect was hired at the start of the project to help Eian characterize the natural features of the property, such as its trees, water runoff patterns, topography—and, of course, solar exposure. The final placement of the home took into account all of these factors. Grading, site disturbance, and tree loss were kept to a minimum. The homeowner personally removed some of the oaks that had to be cut down and had a local mill dry and cut the lumber for later use as stairs, sills, and trim.

In this climate, a Passive House has to be very well insulated, both from the air and from the ground, so one of the first questions that Eian had to address was how to provide the necessary high R-values cost-effectively. He decided to use a combination of 11-inch ICFs for structure and an 11-inch exterior insulation and finish system (EIFS) façade, which was installed directly over the outer shell of the ICF blocks. No drainage plane or ventilation space was required between the two.

ICFs bring significant advantages to the job site. Exterior walls can be put up fairly quickly, with fewer quality control issues to manage than would be the case with traditional wood frame construction. They are also less susceptible to moisture damage, and the continuous layer of concrete creates an airtight shell. Eian specified 25% fly ash, a waste product, as filler for the concrete, to decrease its environmental impact. The interior walls are drywalled and then finished with a beautiful earthen plaster. Altogether, the exterior wall assembly has an overall R-value of almost 75.

The EIFS façade gives the Passive House in the Woods a very clean, modern look. Eian wanted to add a warmer, more receptive feel to the front entry area, so he built a canopy using post-and-beam construction with a corrugated-steel canopy roof. Natural cedar slat siding and porthole openings combine to create a truly welcoming entry.

ICFs bring advantages to the job site, starting with how quickly ICF walls can be created.

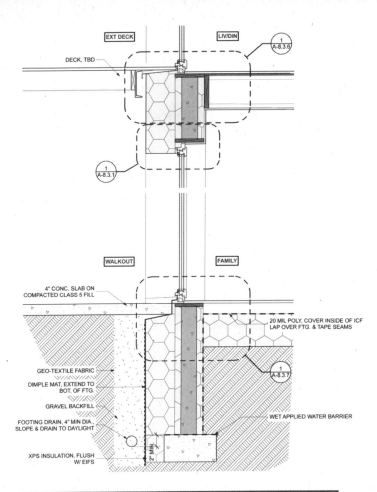

A fundamental question that any PH consultant has to address is how to structure the home's foundation. For this home, the stem walls—the supporting walls between the footings and the exterior walls—which are made from ICFs, sit on frost footings that extend 4 feet below grade. The 4-inch-thick basement slab rests on a sand bed and lots of foam. Morr Construction layered 2-inch boards of high-density foam underneath the center load-bearing footing and 3-inch conventional XPS foam board under the slab to create a 12-inch bed of insulation with an R-value of 60. Since the intersection between the ground below the house and the stem walls amounts to a small surface area, this potential thermal bridge was deemed to be negligible. The basement walls are built in the same way as the above-grade walls, except that the EPS used is a higher-density foam. The finish system on the face is a Sto product that serves as a water barrier and looks like stucco.

To ensure a continuous air barrier, a poly membrane runs across the concrete slab and is sealed to the footings and ICFs, which form the air barrier layer in the vertical walls. The rough openings around the windows and doors were treated with a coat of StoGuard, extending out 1 foot around the opening. The windows were taped to the window bucks with butyl tape, and StoGuard was applied over the insulated gap between the wall and the window frame, to eliminate any avenue for airflow. The window bucks, which were made from FSC-certified timberstrands, were laminated with ice-and-water shield on the side facing the concrete pour, as untreated wood should never directly contact the concrete.

At the top of the house, the heavily insulated flat roof doubles as an outdoor deck with unobstructed sky views. Fourteen-inch I joists and a ¾-inch plywood deck form the support for a Firestone roofing system made of reinforced 60-mil ethylene propylene diene monomer (better known as EPDM) membrane over tapered polyisocyanurate insulation. (That's a mouthful of enes, but EPDM is basically a synthetic rubber compound.) The joints in the

(left) In this climate, a PH has to be very well insulated, both from the air and from the ground. (right) On the first and second floors, two large windows meet to form the southeast corner of the house, allowing light to flood the interior spaces.

plywood decking were taped and sealed with StoGuard, and then the entire surface was painted with it to provide a really secure air barrier layer. With an average of 14 inches of insulation, the R-value for this roof tops out at 95. The EPDM is covered with a fabric protection mat, and layered over that are concrete pavers on pedestals to form the rooftop terrace. The pedestals allow for air to circulate beneath the pavers and promote drying. Warm days in Wisconsin are fleeting, so what better place to draw them out than high atop the house, where the views across the St. Croix River valley are stunning?

For the best views and solar heat gain from inside the house, Eian chose PH-certified, Optiwin Alu2Wood windows. Their insulated frames and triple-pane, low-e-coated GlasTrösch glazing units provide installed R-values of 8 or better. Their SHGC is a high .64, allowing the windows to capture enough solar heat that their heat gains on an annual basis will exceed their losses by better than 50%. On the first and second floors, two of these windows meet to form the southeast corner of the house, allowing light to flood the interior spaces. On each floor, one 3-inch steel column supports the corner structurally. It tucks neatly between the two window frames so as not to obstruct the view. This same tactic—ganging windows

together to maximize light, view, and ventilation—resulted in 30 windows and doors being fitted into 18 rough openings. A mix of operable and fixed units allowed Eian to shave down the window budget a bit, while reducing the number of insect screens that were needed. The operable units were strategically placed to maximize the flow of fresh air through the home during the summer months and minimize heat loss in the winter.

Protecting the building from too much solar heat gain is a precision operation. Exterior aluminum venetian blinds provide shading when it's needed. While each one has its own up-down switch, these blinds are activated by an automated shade controller that has its own dedicated weather station to track solar intensity and wind velocity. The control system is programmed with the location of the house; the date, time, sunrise, and sunset; along with some other user inputs. Compiling all of this information, the unit controls the shades automatically. Wind speeds above 40 mph prompt the controller to retract the blinds to prevent them from getting damaged.

The ventilation and air-conditioning system is another highly efficient operation with an automated component. It consists of a PH-certified, high-efficiency Luefta heat recovery ventilator (HRV), combined with a 600-foot

An exterior insulation and finish system (EIFS) was installed directly over the outer shell of ICF blocks.

cross-linked polyethylene (PEX) tubing loop field, which is buried on the property. The PEX tubing is filled with glycol and connected to a liquid-to-air heat exchanger to preheat or precool and dehumidify the incoming air. The heat exchanger sheds excess humidity through a condensate drain. An automated control system measures indoor CO_2 and humidity and ramps the ventilation system up or down, as needed. By itself, the HRV has a rated heat recovery efficiency of 82%. With the loop field and control system, that efficiency is likely to approach, or even to surpass, 95%.

Thanks to the insulation levels, the airtightness, and all the other building components that make this home a PH, the annual heating load will be less than the heating energy requirement for a PH—in fact, it will beat it by almost 25%. However, in this extremely cold climate, the peak heating load of 19 watts per square meter (W/m^2) can't be met through added heat in the ventilation system alone. The Passivhaus Institut recommends that no more than 10 W/m^2 of heating energy be supplied through the ventilation system. Any higher and the air becomes hot enough that dust will scorch. Therefore, Eian chose a different heating strategy. The entire peak heating load—about 3 kW—will be supplied by electric in-floor heating mats, with local room air thermostats in strategic locations in the bedrooms, the bath, the entry, and the living areas. The energy draw of these heating mats roughly equals that of two hair dryers.

The overall annual source energy performance target for PH will also be met, thanks in part to another efficient heating system—the one that supplies DHW. A 40 ft² solar collector on the roof sends heated water to a 50-gallon storage tank in the mechanical room. It is capable of providing over 80% of the hot water used in the home. A wastewater heat recovery system prewarms the water going into the hot water storage tank, further improving efficiency. When neither method boosts the water temperature to acceptable levels, an electric on-demand water heater kicks into gear and supplies the backup heating. The pipe runs were kept extremely short to reduce heat losses, with all fixtures connected to one centrally located wet wall that runs vertically through the home.

The lighting choices also help to keep electricity use low, with a carefully selected mix of CFLs, LEDs, and halogen lamps. Dimmable halogens are used for spot lighting tasks, CFLs for hallways, and LEDs under the kitchen cabinets. All the exterior fixtures have low-power LED downlights, to minimize light pollution at night; the homeowner's

The homeowner was determined to create a **carbon-neutral, or even a net positive energy, home**. Building to meet the PH standard got him to his goal.

passion is stargazing. One master switch, accessible on the roof, can instantly kill every light on the property.

The garage, which is not built to meet PH standards, butts up against the north side of the house. The two buildings share a common frost footing, but the garage was constructed using advanced stick framing to reduce the total amount of FSC-certified wood being used. To keep the look of the garage consistent with that of the house, Eian specified EIFS for the façade, but with 2 inches, rather than 11 inches, of insulation. There is no interior door connecting the two structures. This eliminates heat loss from the house into the garage and keeps exhaust gases from leaking from the garage into the house. The flat roof of the garage will be filled with sedums, planted in a tray system. This will minimize storm water runoff and create a more pleasant view from the rooftop terrace. The remaining runoff will be captured in rain barrels for use on site.

From the beginning, the homeowner was determined to create a carbon-neutral, or even a net positive energy, home. To meet that goal, he first maximized the energy efficiency of his home, by building to meet the PH standard. Then he chose to install a 3.68kW PV tracker system, as well as a .84kW PV array on the rooftop terrace. Combined, they are expected to generate 6,745 kWh of electricity per year. That's far more than the projected 4,160 kWh that will be used on site, as modeled with the PHPP and assuming two people are living in the house. Generating the excess electricity through PV and selling that excess back to the utility will eliminate the production of 2.9 tons of CO_2 each year, since the utility will not have to generate that amount of electricity using dirtier sources. The homeowner will be using an e-Monitor system from Powerhouse Dynamics to monitor the entire energy balance and compare his home's actual performance to the modeled performance. Eian worked closely with his client to fulfill his vision of a sustainably built, healthy, beautiful home that exceeds even the most stringent of efficiency standards and achieves true carbon neutrality.

PASSIVE HOUSE
Verification Summary

Builder	Morr Construction Services
PH Consultant	Tim Eian
Architect	Tim Eian
City	Hudson, Wisconsin
Year	2010

Specific Space Heat Demand	12 kWh/m²/yr (1.1 kWh/ft²/yr)
Pressurization Test Result	0.6 ACH$_{50}$
Specific Primary Energy Demand (DHW, Heating, Cooling, Auxiliary, and Household Electricity)	68 kWh/m²/yr (6.3 kWh/ft²/yr)
Specific Useful Cooling Energy Demand	1 kWh/m²/yr (0.1 kWh/ft²/yr)

CHAPTER 7

A Community Effort Creates **Affordable Housing**

Western Marin County, California

A pair of barn owls nest in the trees on the corner of the lot. Gently rolling hills are all that is visible from the south-facing windows. Fog, the West Coast's natural air-conditioning, rolls in regularly from the Pacific Ocean to cool warm summer days. On winter mornings, frost sometimes glistens on the grass, but it's gone by the time the sun hits it. This is Northern California—western Marin County, to be exact— where climate problems aren't that problematic. Even here, though, a kilowatt-hour saved is a kilowatt-hour that doesn't have to be generated at a power plant.

The prospect of saving electricity and of cutting carbon emissions by upgrading a planned rental unit to meet the Passive House standard was an appealing one for the board of the nonprofit Community Land Trust Association of West Marin (CLAM). CLAM was established in 2001 to expand housing opportunities in West Marin for low-income residents who work locally. Many of the people who work in West Marin must commute long distances to find affordable housing. Cutting the commute times of those whose work is vital to the local community and reducing their environmental footprint is integral to

CLAM's mission. Still, it took a community effort—builder Terry Nordbye, architect James Bill, and several other PH enthusiasts—to persuade the nonprofit's board to commit to creating housing that would be so energy efficient that utility bills would be affordable for tenants over the long haul. The CLAM rental unit would be the first new-construction PH in California. Transforming this goal into an actual building took an even greater community effort.

Although PH builders often struggle almost equally with problems related to the climate and to the site, site constraints predominated at the CLAM house.

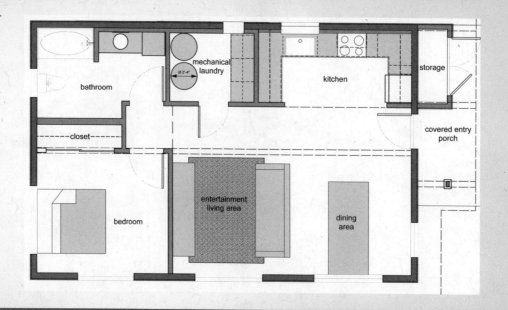

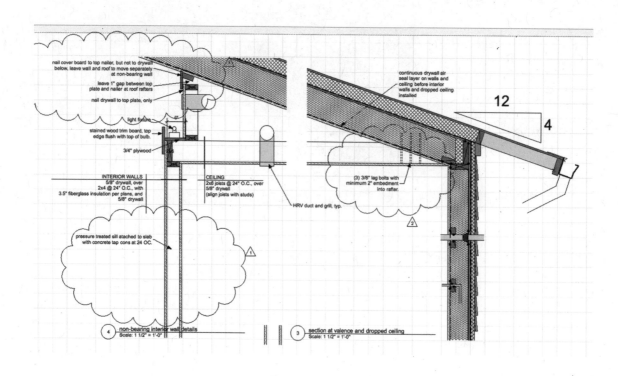

The new tenants—Derek James, Brindi Green, and baby Landon Green James—will get to enjoy a comfortable home with very low utility bills.

Because it is the second unit on a property owned by CLAM, zoning regulations stipulated that the house could be no larger than 750 square feet. And it could be sited only in one specific location. It couldn't be 1 inch further east or north, or it would run into the septic tank and its drainage field. One inch further south or west, and it would violate setback requirements or risk killing the nearby trees. So it could only go exactly where it now stands. It faces 15° off south, but that was a viable constraint in this climate. The small size of the unit presented more of a challenge, since the PH heating and source energy target requirements are measured in energy use per square foot; the smaller the floor area, the less energy that can be used in a given volume for heating, cooling, water heating, lighting, and everything else.

Nordbye is experienced in building energy-efficient homes and even very efficient ones. His first practice run at renovating a home using the PH approach sits just 20 feet away; it's the first unit on this property. He honed his air sealing skills on the first house, and really polished them on the second one.

To guarantee that this new-construction PH would meet the airtightness requirement, a design team that included

Bill, home performance consultant Kevin Beck, and PH consultant Graham Irwin decided that this house would have not just one but two air barrier layers—the sheathing and the drywall. All four walls and both sides of the gable roof are constructed with well-sealed continuous sheets of plywood sheathing on one side of the 2 x 6 framing and drywall on the other. Every penetration through the drywall has blocking behind it, which the plumbing or other penetration is sealed to, and the blocking is sealed with an elastomeric caulk to the drywall. Every puncture, no matter how tiny, is sealed with foam or caulk. The interior partition walls were built after the drywall on the continuous shell was completed, and do not intersect the exterior walls. As much as possible, plumbing and electrical wiring are routed through the interior walls or through an interior furred-out wall that parallels the kitchen and bathroom exterior walls, minimizing the number of holes in the airtight exterior wall assembly.

The exterior walls are filled with 5¼ inches of dense-packed cellulose. A 1-inch layer of rigid XPS blankets the outside of the sheathing and is covered in turn by house wrap. The outermost layer, Hardiplank cement board siding, is held in place by nails that run through the rigid insulation and through the ½-inch plywood into the 2 x 6 studs. The wall assembly was completed with the fiberglass-framed Serious Windows 725 series. On the south-facing side, the windows have the SeriousGlass5, while all the other windows were built with the SeriousGlass9. The windows with the SeriousGlass5 have a higher SHGC, but a lower R-value, than those with the SeriousGlass9. Altogether the exterior walls have an R-value of 30.

The roof was designed with the continuity of the air barrier layer in mind. The main 2 x 8 rafters, which were placed 24 inches OC, are within the thermal boundary. The space between these rafters is filled with 7¼ inches of dense-packed cellulose, which was sprayed in after the drywall was installed. After the cellulose had been packed in, Andy Wahl of AC Building Performance used an IR camera to check that all of the walls and rafters had been completely filled. The rafters are topped with the thoroughly sealed roof sheathing. On top of the shear plywood, another set of rafters, which are offset 12 inches from the main rafters to break any possible thermal bridging, form the eaves. The overhangs are 24 inches,

The gently rolling hills are all that is visible from the south-facing windows.

providing shading for the windows below. These rafters are insulated with 3½ inches of polyisocyanurate insulation snugly packed between them. The polyiso hangs over the plywood on the outside about 1 inch, so that it connects to the rigid foam on the walls. Every piece of foam that was installed was sealed with Touch and Seal foam at all edges and joints, making a continuous foam layer from the roof to the foundation. The total R-value of the roof assembly is 50.

Figuring out how to construct a foundation that would be thermally isolated from the ground was another challenging design task, which Bill solved with much help from structural engineer Katy Hollbacher. They came up with a design in which the concrete slab is surrounded on five sides by foam. Below the slab is 7 inches of XPS foam, creating an insulating layer with an R-value of 35. The underslab foam connects up with 2 inches of polyiso foam installed between the slab and the concrete stem wall that forms the perimeter of the building. Another stem wall supports the middle of the building.

Nordbye is a self-confessed compulsive air sealer, which he says is a highly desirable characteristic for anyone who wants to build a house that meets the PH airtightness requirement. He did his best to train his crew to be as compulsive and careful as he is about not interrupting the air barrier layer. Still, there were times when Nordbye would leave the site for an hour and come back and find a hole somewhere. He jokes that every worker who touches the house is a potential disaster. More seriously, an airtight home requires constant supervision by someone who is continuously on site to make sure that no holes are created that aren't properly sealed. Nordbye's attentiveness to details paid off. The final blower door test, which was conducted by George Nesbitt, of House as a System, came in at 41 CFM_{50} or 0.36 ACH_{50}. After the test, Nordbye found a 2-inch hole in the electrical panel, where the electrical service comes into the house, that he quickly sealed, making the house even tighter.

To bring fresh air into the home when the windows are closed, Bill specified installing an UltimateAir ERV, which claims a heat transfer efficiency of 95%. Heat for the home will be supplied predominantly by a solar-water-heated water-to-air heat exchanger that is in line with the ERV's

This area gets plenty of sunshine over the year, turning the nearby hills brown in early summer.

duct system. The solar water heating system consists of four rooftop-mounted panels through which potable water is pumped and heated, and two 80-gallon storage tanks that are plumbed in parallel. Since the system was sized to supply both heat and hot water, it is massively oversized for the summer months, when the tenants will need it only to provide domestic hot water. To avoid overheating the water and possibly damaging the system, Bill chose a fully automated drain-back system that will drain the water out of the panels when the water in the storage tanks is already sufficiently hot. In winter, the system will send water up to the panels if the panel temperature exceeds the temperature of the water in the storage tanks, thus ensuring that the water in the panels will never freeze. When the tenants need heat, a sensor in the storage tanks will turn on the pump that sends hot water from the storage tanks to the heat exchanger in the ducts. If there isn't enough solar-heated water to provide heat, a backup electric element in the ducts will turn on. Sun First Solar donated the labor required to install the solar-thermal system. The panels and

tanks were provided at cost by Vaillant Solar Systems, who also donated solar consulting and modeling time.

There is a backup heating system for the DHW as well, should there be too many cloudy or rainy days in a row. When a tenant turns on the hot water, water flows from the solar storage tank to a 20-gallon electric water heater. If the water arriving at the water heater is cooler than 120°F, the electric water heater will turn on and boost the water's temperature. All of this technology is automated and will be invisible to the tenants, who will only have to know that heat and hot water are always available.

Since this area gets plenty of sunny days over the year, very little fossil fuel should be needed to provide DHW. Yet Bill and Nordbye went even one step further to maximize the efficiency of the water heating system: They had a Metlund on-demand pump installed at the kitchen sink. Once activated, this pump sends the cold water that has been sitting in the pipes leading up to the faucet back to the solar storage tank until hot water arrives at the faucet. When the hot water arrives, the pump turns itself off. With this pump, the cold water doesn't just run down the drain

The house represents the symbiosis between the two certifications —energy efficiency and the environmental impact of the materials used in the home.

Rae Levine, outgoing executive director of CLAM, thanks all who contributed to the creation of the organization's newest rental unit. To her left stand builder Terry Nordbye and architect James Bill, and to her right is CLAM's new executive director, Sam Leguizamon Grant.

and get wasted, as usually happens, while the homeowner waits for hot water to arrive at the faucet. Even in a small house, where the distance between the water heater and the faucet is short, a few quarts of water can be wasted waiting for the hot water to arrive—and a few quarts each time quickly turns into several gallons a day disappearing down the drain.

Water efficiency is not directly accounted for in the PH certification process, but it does affect LEED certification, which Bill has applied for with consultant Prudence Ferreira. Bill is excited about the symbiosis between the two certifications that the house represents; the first emphasizes energy efficiency, while the second emphasizes concern for the environmental impact of the materials used in the home. All of the wood used is either FSC-certified or salvaged lumber. All of the finishes are water based, and the paints contain no VOCs. The concrete floor was troweled smooth, and finished with a water-based stain and a clear coat. Although Nordbye was the general contractor on this project, the completion of the PH depended on generous donations of time, materials, and money from a whole host of community members—too many to mention. Fairfax Lumber supplied many of the green construction materials at cost. Nordbye made no profit on his services and Bill donated his time. And the volunteer efforts haven't ended with the completion of the house. Every electrical circuit in the house is connected to a data logger, so that data on energy consumption can be collected on a monthly basis.

CLAM also hopes to collect and analyze data on indoor temperature and humidity, along with the performance of the solar system.

With the many donations and volunteer efforts, it is difficult for Nordbye to determine the exact cost of the house. When Bill has a spare moment, he will work with a construction estimator, Paul Waszink, to figure out the likely cost per square foot and compare that to what it would have cost to build a comparable house that met California's energy code, as well as performing a life cycle and carbon reduction cost-benefit analysis. Nordbye estimates that, including the value of the volunteer labor and donated materials, the house cost roughly $330/ft². Although that may seem high, Nordbye says it's a low figure for a custom house in Marin County, where costs generally start at $400/ft² and shoot up from there. In addition, small houses tend to cost more on a per square foot basis than larger houses do.

For Bill and Nordbye, the education and experience of designing and constructing a PH made the loss of profit on their services well worth it. They enjoyed having to tinker and be PH pioneers, and they loved getting to know all the volunteers who contributed their labor. This PH was a community effort, and it will benefit the community as well. The tenants who moved in recently work locally, but they used to live in Petaluma—a half-hour commute back and forth every day, burning fossil fuels and spewing emissions. That was so last century.

PASSIVE HOUSE
Verification Summary

Builder	Terry Nordbye		Specific Space Heat Demand	11.5 kWh/m²/yr (1.1 kWh/ft²/yr)
PH Consultant	Lowell Moulton		Pressurization Test Result	0.36 ACH$_{50}$
Architect	James Bill		Specific Primary Energy Demand (DHW, Heating, Cooling, Auxiliary, and Household Electricity)	117.8 kWh/m²/yr (10.9 kWh/ft²/yr)
City	Western Marin County, California			
Year	2010		Specific Useful Cooling Energy Demand	1 kWh(m²/yr (0.1 kWh/ft²/yr)

CHAPTER 8

Transforming
a Family Home

Portland, Oregon

Tad Everhart is neither a builder nor a developer, but he used to be. For six years he built homes and developed properties in Portland, Oregon. In 1998, he and his brother, who remains a builder, developed the subdivision and built the house that Everhart now lives in with his family. Everhart became a lawyer who helps nonprofits, such as affordable-housing organizations, with their legal issues. Still, he knows houses and couldn't shake his sense of responsibility for how the operation of his house was affecting the global climate. In 2008, he stumbled across some articles about the Passive House concept, and got so intrigued that he signed up for the first PH consultant training.

That was the first step in redoing what was admittedly a fairly new, fairly energy-efficient home already. For Everhart, given the reality of climate change, a fairly efficient home just wasn't enough.

The PH consultant training further convinced Everhart that he had found the right approach to reducing his family's carbon emissions. He toyed briefly with selling the house he had built just ten years earlier and building a new one, but that tactic didn't sit right with him for several reasons. Since the PH standard represents the best, most realistic energy use for a home, it made sense to Everhart that his own home should become a model of how houses can be retrofitted to meet that standard. Otherwise, how could he hope to convince others to do

likewise? In addition, his family likes the house and the neighborhood that he developed. All the homes face onto a quiet cul-de-sac, which the neighborhood kids easily cross as they migrate from house to house. Plus, the area is transit friendly, with nearby buses that feed into the light-rail system that crisscrosses Portland. Finally, he couldn't afford the cost of buying a lot and building a new home, although he could get a home equity loan to help cover the retrofit costs. He knew that retrofitting wouldn't exactly be cheap, and it would be much more difficult than new construction, but it was the best, most practical option.

Having made the decision to retrofit, Everhart next had to figure out the best approach. He weighed adding insulation and thickening the walls from the inside

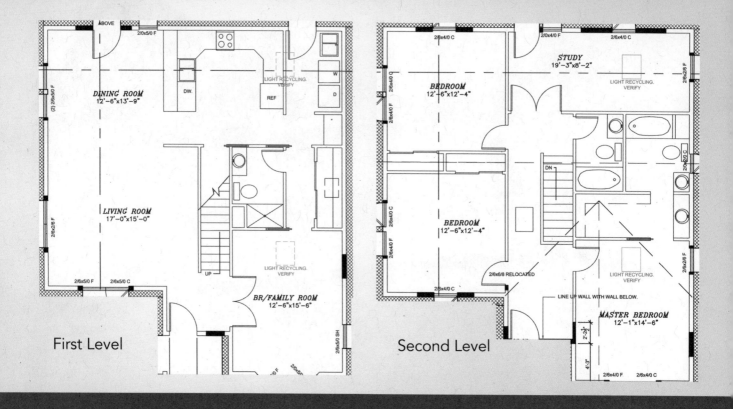

First Level

Second Level

against an exterior strategy. At first the interior approach seemed good. His house is a bit larger than what his family needs, so losing some interior space would be fine. Still, retrofitting from the inside would require redoing walls that were better left alone, such as the one holding all the kitchen cabinets. It also would require narrowing an entry hallway, which would reduce accessibility. Approaching the retrofit from the exterior would mean less of an intrusion into his family's living space and—he hoped—into their ability to live in the home during the construction process.

Adding insulation from the exterior thickens the walls of a house, so they take up more of a given lot. Everhart's neighborhood was an infill development ten years ago, and the homes are all fairly close to one another. Five-foot setbacks are required, and most homes just meet that requirement. Everhart's house was the exception, with a 6-foot setback, an attribute that Everhart felt was providential. Twelve inches was just about what he would need. Besides, redoing the exterior would allow him to correct the one possibly serious mistake he felt he had made when the home was built. Only afterward did Everhart hear about rain screen construction. Creating a

rain screen layer just under the siding helps block wind-driven rain from getting into the wall assembly, which can lead to water damage and rot in the walls. In an area where drizzle, showers, and downpours are routine, not having a rain screen is about as practical as never wearing a raincoat while working outdoors every day. During Portland's winter, when the rain and wind-driven moisture can be relentless—there are 222 days without sunshine every year—the exterior walls just don't get enough sun to dry out.

When he looked at the existing 12-inch overhangs, he saw another makeover opportunity. In winter, larger overhangs would shelter more of the siding; in summer, they would create more shade. Everhart added this feature to his must-change list.

Tackling a retrofit from the exterior presents its own challenges. Pondering these, Everhart remembered an article that he had read in Fine Homebuilding describing a Larsen truss—essentially an outer, nonstructural wall that consists of a lightweight framework, or truss, filled with insulation. Then he attended a presentation about panelized wall systems in European PHs, and realized that

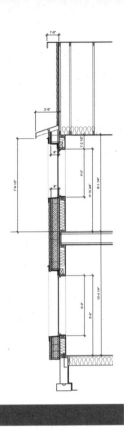

he could meld the two concepts to create what he needed. His overall strategy became: take off the existing cedar siding, which he wanted to reuse; air seal the existing sheathing; surround the house with Larsen trusses; install nonstructural sheathing over them; install building wrap and rain screen battens; and put the original cedar siding back on.

Great plan, said his brother, who had volunteered to be the general contractor and donate his time, except for that part about reusing the siding. Couldn't be done, he said, because the existing cedar siding couldn't be removed without destroying it. But Everhart persisted. Not only did he like his siding, but he wasn't enthusiastic about the likely substitute—fiber cement siding.

Yes, it's durable; but too much electricity was used, and too many carbon emissions were created, during its production for Everhart's comfort. Besides, the much-greater weight of fiber cement siding would complicate the Larsen truss design and construction (and compromise the house in an earthquake). Everhart encouraged the carpenters he had worked with for years to experiment with four or five different removal techniques. They did, and eventually they figured out a way to pop the nails off without damaging the siding too much. Everhart estimates that they managed to rescue and reuse about 50% of the siding. The boards that weren't in good enough condition to reuse were donated to local carpenters making chicken coops.

Once the siding had been removed, the crew set to work on creating a continuous air barrier layer—always a challenge in a retrofit. Air sealing the existing ½-inch plywood sheathing with flashing tape—primarily Grace Vycor Plus—required tenacity and careful attention to detail, but it was a fairly straightforward process. The tape was used to cover all horizontal and vertical seams in the plywood, as well as the nail holes. The Larsen trusses, which are screwed to the building at the studs, squeeze the

tape against the vertical seams of the plywood sheathing, reinforcing the seal. Where there were horizontal seams, the crew taped them and stapled strips of plywood over them to keep the tape tight against the seams. To extend the air barrier downward, Everhart and his crew applied a layer of silicone sealant to the inside of the plywood sheathing to seal it to the bottom plate and then used backer rod and more silicone to seal the bottom plate to the floor's plywood sheathing.

Reducing envelope penetrations as much as possible took planning and flexibility. The Everharts' home did not have a conventional fireplace and chimney, but it did have a direct-vent gas fireplace with a standing pilot light. Removing that appliance not only allowed Everhart to seal up a large hole, but also shut down the wasteful carbon emissions from the pilot light. Besides, according to Everhart's Passive House Planning Package (PHPP) calculations, the gas fireplace would produce more heat than would be needed to meet the family's peak heating load. Moving the gas dryer to the garage eliminated two holes in the envelope (gas pipe through floor and vent through exterior wall). Removing the gas dryer created a space for an interior clothes-drying closet, where warm air that is being exhausted from the house by the heat recovery ventilator (HRV) will help to remove the moisture from freshly washed clothes spread out on a drying rack. They eliminated another ten penetrations for electrical wires by rerouting wires and consolidating them into a single sleeved penetration, and they eliminated two of five water supply penetrations.

Using the PHPP software, Everhart figured out that he would need to fill the Larsen trusses with 10 inches of dense-packed cellulose insulation to meet the PH energy performance target, given Portland's climate. In addition to the cellulose-filled Larsen truss, the new wall assembly is sheathed on the outside with ½-inch nonstructural Celotex fiberboard. A layer of Tyvek covers the fiberboard, and ³/₈-inch El Dorado plastic battens are screwed into the fiberboard. These plastic battens create the rain screen gap—and incidentally provide a bit of a thermal break. Together with the 5½ inches of fiberglass already in the 2 x 6 stud walls, the new wall assembly would have an overall R-value of 50.

Unfortunately those fiberglass batts turned out to be poorly installed. Although he had planned not to touch

The front, east-facing side of the house could only be thickened by 2 inches, so Everhart added 2 inches of EPS to the outside and another 7 inches of XPS on the interior.

much of the interior, Everhart ended up removing, replacing, or reconfiguring all of the windows. When the Sheetrock around the windows was removed, he discovered big voids in the fiberglass insulation, spots where moisture had caused it to decay a bit already, and areas where air movement had brought in enough dust to turn the insulation brown. Since he had already pulled the Sheetrock off about half of the exterior walls, he decided to go ahead and remove another 25% of the Sheetrock. With access to almost all of the exterior wall framing, he was able to eliminate or reduce headers, trimmers, Sheetrock nailers, and other unnecessary framing, which cut the wood-insulation ratio to almost the equivalent of what would be found in an advanced-framing wall. He also added the El Dorado battens and Insulcap aerogel to the inside of the framing for an additional thermal break. Then his insulation installer blew cellulose into every 2 x 6 bay that he had access to and every joist bay on the second floor, to deaden sound transmission. The new wall assembly now has a total R-value of 51.

The Everharts like windows, especially in winter, when the Willamette Valley is gray and overcast 90% of the time. They like them so much that before the retrofit, they had 33 windows and two glass patio doors. To cut heat loss and meet the PH performance target, Everhart needed to reduce the overall rough opening of the glazing component from 508 to 242 square feet. Instead of the original 33 windows, he bought 17 windows that he strategically placed to optimize light, ventilation, and access. Because many of the new windows are fixed with low-profile, thin frames, there is less reduction in glazing than there might otherwise have been. All of the new, operable windows are casements, which provide about as much ventilation as the house used to have. Everhart had wanted low-e, argon-filled, triple-glazed replacement windows, for their performance and promised durability. Unfortunately he was unable to find a window manufacturer willing to supply argon-filled windows to Portland. Seeking the highest-performance windows that he could afford, Everhart chose the Serious Windows 925 series with high solar gain, which have an R-value of more than 7, but a solar heat gain coefficient (SHGC) of only 0.42. A higher SHGC that would let in more solar heat would have been preferable.

The patio doors were replaced by two new all-glass doors made by Innotech, a Canadian firm. Each of these doors has triple-pane, tempered glass with an unplasticized vinyl frame that has a steel channel running through it to add stiffness. (Plasticizing PVC is an extremely toxic

After the installation of the dense-packed cellulose insulation is finished, the new wall assembly will have an overall R-value of 51.

process, and unplasticized PVC, while rare in the United States, is popular in Europe, where it is considered very green.) The doors have three separate rubber seals and cams on all four edges to hold them tightly to the frame like a casement window. They are also heavy, weighing in at 220 pounds apiece. The front door, which faces the street, was not replaced, so that it would continue to match the doors of the other homes in the development.

The front, east-facing side of the house presented another challenge: The required setback from the street meant that Everhart could thicken the walls on the exterior by only 2 inches. For this façade he added 2 inches of XPS to the exterior and another 7 inches of XPS on the interior, creating a wall assembly with an R-value of 45.

Everhart's plans for the topmost layer of his house—replacing his current asphalt roof with a cooler, reflective metal one—ran into serious opposition from his neighbors, who objected to its potential glare. To keep the peace, the roof mostly remains as it was, but the west-facing half of the roof, which is not visible from any of the neighbors' homes, was painted with a reflective coating. New and improved overhangs extend out 2 feet and, combined with the 4 inches of gutter, provide 28 inches of shading on the south, west, and part of the east sides.

Everhart plans to plant a cherry tree on the east side of the house to provide food and shade as his Mediterranean prune tree presently does on the south side. Trees kick in additional seasonal shading on the east side of his house. On the south side, Everhart relies on a less-conventional method—scarlet runner beans, kiwis, and other annual and perennial vines. He plants the fast-growing scarlet runner beans in June. By the beginning of August, they are usually 10 feet tall, and by the end of that month, they gain another 20 feet and are knocking on the roof. In addition to providing shade, these plants produce beautiful orange flowers that attract hummingbirds and bumblebees. The west side features another appetizing plant—the kiwi. It's an old-fashioned strategy, but it successfully cuts down on summertime overheating, while providing some appealing side benefits.

The wintertime heating solution doesn't have quite the same sensory appeal, but it has real benefits and charm. The Everharts chose to get a Zehnder America ComfoAir 350, the first one of these HRVs to be sold in North America. Like any HRV, the unit brings in fresh supply air from outside at a steady rate, exhausts the stale air, and transfers heat from the exhaust to the supply air. This unit ventilates at a rate of from 80 to 215 CFM,

Looking at his house with a 100-year time line in mind, Everhart wants to have no regrets—and for him that will only be possible if he makes his home as **efficient and as durable** as he can right now.

To cut heat loss, Everhart reduced the number of windows in his house from 33 to 17, which he placed strategically to optimize light and ventilation.

depending on the setting, while transferring up to 90% of the heat in the exhausted air to the incoming supply air. Fresh air is distributed throughout the house through flexible high-density polyethylene (HDPE) pipes 3 inches in diameter. The Everharts supplemented this system with an electric-resistance in-line heater. The HRV is so quiet at its all-day lowest setting that it is barely noticeable, say the Everharts. They have the HRV programmed to ratchet up to the medium-flow setting for two 90-minute periods, one in the morning and one at night. If they are cooking up a storm and showering, they turn it up manually to the highest setting. The heating system is programmed to maintain a temperature of 68°F throughout the day, and

that's what it does. The Everharts don't notice how often, or even whether, the in-line heater is kicking in to warm the ventilation air. What they do notice is how comfortable they now are in their home during the winter.

At the time that they bought their HRV, Zehnder had not yet obtained a UL listing for it, so the Everharts had to go before a newly created Alternative Technology Advisory Committee (ATAC) that considers exceptions to the building permit process involving new technologies. ATAC, which is staffed by volunteer engineers, architects, and green builders, approved the installation. The Everharts were the first to appear before the committee and are also its first repeat customers. They returned to seek approval for installing seven air admittance valves, which are energy-efficient substitutes for plumbing vent stacks that penetrate the roof. An air admittance valve consists of a tightly sealed, one-way cap that allows air to enter the vent stack only when the plumbing is in use, and is otherwise tightly shut so that no sewer gases can escape into the home. Vent stacks with these valves only have to extend above the trap, not all the way through the roof, thus avoiding the energy penalty associated with a roof penetration.

One energy penalty that Everhart wasn't able to avoid was the thermal bridge in the joint between the exterior walls and the foundation. Everhart's exterior walls sit directly on a ¾-inch plywood subfloor, which rests on a mudsill, which sits on the concrete foundation. The solid wood resting on top of the concrete creates a thermal bridge that Everhart couldn't address directly. He had contemplated lifting the house off the foundation to insert a layer of high-density XPS foam to interrupt the thermal bridge. But the bids he got—one was $15,000, and the other was $16,000—were beyond his budget, and neither bid included rebuilding the foundation. Instead, he compensated for the energy penalty by reducing window sizes, especially on the north side.

The shallow crawl space presented a more-serious challenge to Everhart's problem-solving abilities. In order to stop heat migrating from the house to the crawl space—and have a warm floor underfoot—he would have to figure out how to insulate cost-effectively below the ground floor. The 2 x 10 joists that hold up his lower floor were insulated with poorly installed fiberglass batts. Those would have to go. In their place, Everhart installed precut expanded polystyrene (EPS) blocks, 17½ inches wide by 10 inches high by 4 feet long, sized to fit snugly between the joists, which are 19.2 inches OC, and to fit within the through-floor access hatch. The blocks are held in place by short finishing nails driven through the joists and spray foam, which Everhart applied to fill the small gaps between the blocks and the joists. Previously, he had carefully sealed the plywood subfloor to create the first layer of the air barrier. To create the second layer, he stapled two sheets of Insul-Cap, a ³/₈-inch-thick blanket of a very-high-R-value product, to the bottom of the joists with a thin strip of lath. The final layer of the air barrier was made of three sheets of a ¾-inch-thick R-tech Fanfold rigid EPS insulation with a foil facing, with all seams staggered and taped with a foil tape. The overall ground floor assembly has an R-value of 49.

The whole retrofit process has been a long haul for Everhart—seven months and counting, at press time. Although most of the work is done, Everhart isn't finished yet. His most recent blower door result was 850 CFM. He plans to further reduce air leakage in his home to meet the newly created PH retrofit standard of 1.0 ACH$_{50}$. The total cost for this retrofit has been about $120,000. Everhart is really grateful to his brother for helping him out by donating his services as a general contractor. While it was expensive, Everhart thinks that this project has been the best use of his money. Looking at his house with a 100-year time line in mind, he wants to have no regrets—and for him that will only be possible if he makes his home as efficient and as durable as he can right now.

PASSIVE HOUSE
Verification Summary

Builder	Tad Everhart
PH Consultant	Tad Everhart
Designer	Tad Everhart
City	Portland, Oregon
Year	2010

Specific Space Heat Demand	4.57 kBtu/ft²/yr (1.3 kWh/ft²/yr)
Pressurization Test Result	0.6 ACH$_{50}$*
Specific Primary Energy Demand (DHW, Heating, Cooling, Auxiliary, and Household Electricity)	26.7 kBtu/ft²/yr (7.9 kWh/ft²/yr)
Specific Useful Cooling Energy Demand	4.75 kBtu/ft²/yr (1.4 kWh/ft²/yr)

*target

CHAPTER 9

Sustainability and Preservation—Twin Goals for a Retrofit

Brooklyn, New York

Brownstones are quintessential Brooklyn row houses, an architectural chapter that originated in the 19th century, when a brown sandstone was readily available from quarries located in New Jersey and Connecticut. They also represent coveted opportunities—each one a chance to live in a house in New York City. What they generally aren't is energy efficient, but one four-story brownstone in the Park Slope area of Brooklyn has become the exception after a Passive House retrofit shepherded by PH consultant and architect Jeremy Shannon of Prospect Architecture in collaboration with PH consultant David White of Right Environments.

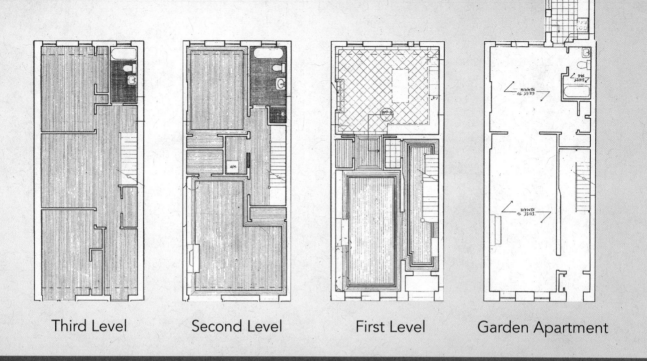

| Third Level | Second Level | First Level | Garden Apartment |

On the exterior façade, the original carvings still grace this brownstone. On the inside, many original details also remain, including the arched stained-glass windows, mahogany casement trim, and staircase moldings. Measuring just 21 feet by 45 feet, the building houses a garden-level apartment, an upper triplex, and a full cellar that connects to the triplex. And apparently many leaks. The first blower door test, before any retrofit work had begun, came in at 8,500 CFM_{50}. To achieve the PH airtightness standard would require dropping the leakiness of the building to just 300 CFM_{50}. Shannon and his construction manager, James Flugger, had their work cut out for them.

Like many brownstones in Park Slope, this building has acquired a landmark status, which means that any change that Shannon contemplated had to be approved by the board of the New York City Landmark Commission. Getting approval to install windows that performed well enough to meet the PH standard was an early and daunting task—but Shannon and White succeeded in the end. They presented information to the commission about PH, including a copy of *Homes for a Changing Climate: Passive Houses in the U.S.* The commission members were excited

about the opportunity this project presented to showcase preservation efforts that would result in a more-sustainable building. They granted unanimous approval to Shannon's plan to upgrade window performance in the building by installing customized, German-manufactured Optiwin windows, including some that featured an inset tilt-and-turn lower sash with a fixed upper sash made to simulate the historic double-hung windows. The commission awarded its approval largely because Shannon pledged to do everything he could to match the outward appearance of the original windows.

It was a simply worded pledge, but complying with it meant clearing some major hurdles. Most importantly, the frames of the new triple-pane windows that Shannon would be ordering were going to be much thicker than the old ones. This meant that he would have to take very careful measurements, and do some tricky calculations, so that the old interior window shutters and casements could be refurbished and reinstalled, and still fit properly. Three badly damaged stained-glass windows presented another series of hurdles. They were sent to a local stained-glass shop for repairs, but since the damage was so extensive, the repairs were going to take at least four weeks. Since

Shannon ordered customized window frames and glass to preserve the original look of the windows, but significantly upgrade their performance.

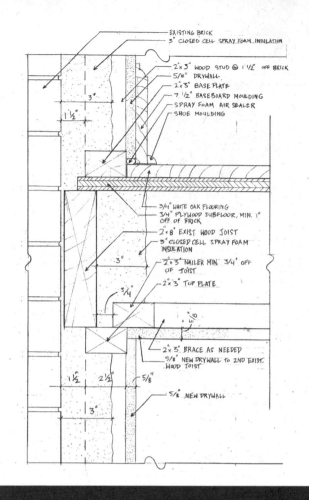

EXISTING BRICK
3" CLOSED CELL SPRAY FOAM INSULATION
2"x 3" WOOD STUD @ 1 1/2" OFF BRICK
5/8" DRYWALL
2"x 3" BASE PLATE
7 1/2" BASEBOARD MOULDING
SPRAY FOAM AIR SEALER
SHOE MOULDING
3/4" WHITE OAK FLOORING
3/4" PLYWOOD SUBFLOOR, MIN. 1" OFF OF BRICK
2"x 8" EXIST WOOD JOIST
3" CLOSED CELL SPRAY FOAM INSULATION
2"x 3" NAILER MIN. 3/4" OFF OF JOIST
2"x 3" TOP PLATE
2"x 3" BRACE AS NEEDED
5/8" NEW DRYWALL TO 2ND EXIST. WOOD JOIST
5/8" NEW DRYWALL

Shannon didn't have the luxury of being able to wait four weeks to order the customized Optiwin window frames and glass, he had to get a template made of the stained glass without the frame and send that to Germany. Once the stained glass was fixed, it was crated and shipped directly to Germany to be fitted onto the Optiwin windows. For two of these windows, the stained glass was fixed with silicon onto the front frame of the window, sealing it in place so its full beauty would be visible from the outside—and meeting the landmark requirements. The third stained-glass window was custom-inserted into a triple-pane window frame, forming the middle pane. According to Shannon, Optiwin was incredibly helpful during the design and production of these custom windows.

Finding better-performing replacements for the two existing skylights posed yet another set of challenges.

Shannon did a thorough search of all U.S. window manufacturers for skylights that would meet PH standards. He couldn't find any that even came close. Nor could he find a German company that would ship high-performing skylights to the United States. Finally, another PH consultant told him about Fakro, a Polish company that does ship very high-performing, wood-framed skylights to this country. Although the Fakro skylights are not Passivhaus Institute certified, they are far better than anything else Shannon was able to find, having a frame U-value of .16 and a glass U-value of .09. The client appreciates these skylights for how easily they tilt open and closed, as well as for the look of their natural wood frames.

Once Shannon had won the landmark commission's approval, the work to rehab this brownstone from the inside could begin. The brownstone that characterizes these

On the parlor floor a staircase that is finished with beautifully detailed raised-panel mahogany trim hugs the east-facing wall.

This badly damaged stained-glass window was repaired, shipped to Germany, and then custom fitted onto a high-performance window.

row houses is actually just a veneer over brick walls. In this building, the brick is laid in three courses to form the back wall and in four courses to form the front wall. Inside the front and back walls are framing members that provide a chase for plumbing and electrical wires. The interior side of the framing is covered with drywall. The walls that abut the neighbors' homes—the party walls—are constructed of brick, covered on the inside with lath and plaster. The first step in the retrofit work was to gain access to the brick, so that a continuous layer of insulation could be installed from the cellar to the roof. But when Shannon took down the drywall, he discovered a range of unexpected problems—from broken header beams to cut joists to cloth wiring—all of which had to be addressed before the insulation could be applied.

For the insulating layer, Shannon chose to rely on a soy-based spray foam, since it would not only insulate but also help to create a continuous air barrier. His plan was to cover most of the front and back walls, as well as 3 feet of the party walls on either side, with 3¼ inches of foam to yield an R-value of 21.5. Before the spraying could begin, the carpenters installed a lot of bracing on the studs of the framed walls to keep them from moving out of plumb or level when the foam expanded.

After the initial spray, it was clear that there were problem areas. In some places, there just wasn't enough room for adequate amounts of foam. One such place was where a partition wall ran perpendicular to the exterior wall framing, and there was too much wood and little to no foam. Shannon solved this problem by having the exterior wall studs removed, filling in the area where the studs had been with spray foam, and then installing a nailer for the drywall. Other areas simply looked as if they hadn't been adequately covered, so Shannon developed a simple method to determine whether this was the case. He cut small bamboo skewers into 3-inch lengths and stuck them into the sprayed-on foam every couple of feet, or wherever the foam looked low. If the foam didn't cover the skewer, the installers sprayed that area again. Bamboo does not act as a thermal bridge, so the skewers could be left in place and sprayed right over.

After the insulation installers had filled in the problem areas, Shannon ran a blower door test. The disappointingly high results inspired him to pull out an IR camera. Since IR cameras record temperature differences, and since this work was taking place during a cold New York winter, he had the crew first warm the house with temporary heaters to 50°F to 60°F. Then they turned on a blower door to draw in outside air, which was roughly 30°F. The IR camera quickly identified air leaks, demonstrating that the spray foam insulation was not providing a continuous air barrier, as Shannon had expected. There were holes in the middle of the foamed areas, even where the foam was 3 inches deep, and leaks at many of the corners as well. Using a low-VOC spray paint, they marked all the leaky places, and the insulation contractors gradually filled them in.

At first Shannon thought he might not have to air seal the brick party walls. In most brownstones, plaster was applied directly onto the brick, which prevents air from moving through the walls. However, in this building the brick had been overlaid with lath, and the plaster had been applied over the lath, creating convenient channels for air movement. Wherever the party walls were accessible, Shannon had the lath removed, and Flugger hand-rolled these areas with StoGuard Gold, an elastomeric coating. Flugger decided not to treat the east-facing party wall on the parlor floor, which is hugged by a staircase that is finished with beautifully detailed raised-panel mahogany trim.

Maintaining a continuous air boundary into the cellar was a very complex process. The cellar floor and walls had to be watertight as well as airtight, since the clients planned to use the cellar as a work space. To begin with, the contracting crew moved gas lines, meters, and electrical panels off the inside of the cellar's front wall, which was constructed of stone, so that a continuous layer of insulation could be installed behind it. Then they excavated the old cracked slab, digging down an additional 12 inches, but taking care not to dig below the footings, so

that a proper drainage detail could be incorporated into the new slab. They dug three narrow trenches that ran parallel to the party walls and 10 inches deeper than the overall excavation and gently sloped the rest of the ground toward these trenches. They then tamped the earth to reduce future settling. Next, they lowered 6-inch percolating pipes made from HDPE with recycled content into the trenches. The pipes were gravity pitched to the sump pump in the front of the house. The trenches and pitched earth were then covered with 2 or 3 inches of gravel, which was also tamped down. They framed out the cellar walls with 2 x 3 studs spaced 1½ inches off of the brick cellar walls and 6 inches from the level line of the gravel floor. They then covered the gravel floor with 2 inches of the soy-based spray foam insulation and continued up the walls, covering them with a continuous 3-inch layer of foam. Finally, they laid a 4-inch concrete slab over the insulation on the cellar floor, raising the height of the floor to the level of the studs. Sound-dampening 5/8-inch Quiet Rock drywall, mounted on spring tracks, was installed over the insulation on the walls.

At the front and back of the house, small access areas abut the cellar. These areas were probably once used to bring coal or other supplies into the brownstone. Shannon isolated these spaces, keeping them outside the thermal boundary of the building. Each access area has its own separate slab and drain. Shannon had the spray foam brought up between the access slabs and the cellar slab to eliminate any possibility of thermal bridging there. Custom-made insulated doors at each opening guard against heat transmission across this boundary.

A single-floor addition that was new about 100 years ago further complicated this retrofit. Grafted onto the back of the building, this roughly 150 ft² room had become a kitchen for the garden apartment, and it still looked to be in pretty good shape at the start of this project. Since that was the case, the clients originally weren't interested in remodeling this space—an understandable preference, but one that created complications, because it meant Shannon would have to figure out a way to keep the addition outside the thermal boundary of the building. Unfortunately for the clients, who had recently purchased the brownstone, the addition suffered damage during a storm, and when Shannon went to repair the damage, he found rot on the underside of the addition's roof deck. The clients changed their minds and decided to include the addition in the retrofit. The new four-ply bituminous rollout roof, roof deck, roof joists, and waterproofing membrane should keep water out of the addition for at least 20 years. While this work was being done, the interior side of the roof deck was sprayed with 8 or more inches of foam to achieve an R-value of 60. Shannon also added 3¼ inches of spray foam to the interior side of the walls that were exposed during the reconstruction of the addition.

The slab under the addition was still in good shape, which was unfortunate from a PH renovation perspective. To keep the whole building warm, this slab should have been insulated from the ground, but this would have meant tearing out the old slab and replacing it with a new one, and the clients didn't want to have a good slab go to waste. Instead, Shannon specified topping it with 2 inches of Dow Thermax, a rigid polyiso insulation. Two 4-foot by 8-foot sheets of ½-inch plywood, laid crosswise over each other, cover the insulation and provide support for the final layer of ³/₄-inch oak flooring, creating a slightly springy floating floor. The 100-year-old addition was transformed into a comfortable, inviting kitchen.

The best way to achieve the desired airtightness for this building would have been to install the windows first, and test for any remaining leaks before closing up the walls. Shannon was not able to do this because he couldn't stop the retrofit work while he waited for the windows to arrive from Germany. Instead, he completed as much sealing as possible, installed most of the drywall, covered the rough window openings with plastic film, and then ran another blower door test. He still got unacceptably high leakage. Puzzled, he and White turned to longtime energy expert Marc Rosenbaum for advice.

Rosenbaum recommended figuring out how much of the leakage was actually going to the outside—and not just through the party walls. He reasoned that any leakage through the party walls didn't represent actual heat loss, since both neighbors were conditioning their homes. Acting on this advice, Shannon and White conducted a dual blower door test by first depressurizing the house

The kitchen was thoroughly updated and will be a warm and cozy venue for family meals.

they were working on and then, with another blower door, depressurizing first one and then the other neighbor's house. (He offered free energy audits to the neighbors to win their consent.) When Shannon turned on the second blower door in the first neighbor's house, leakage to that house was 650 CFM_{50}. When he repeated this test, this time with the second blower door installed in the second neighbor's house, leakage to that house was 200 CFM_{50}. Rosenbaum advised Shannon that he could subtract the 850 CFM_{50} of leakage through the party walls from his overall leakage. The remaining 1,050 CFM_{50} represented the true energy leakage in the PH. Discussions with PHIUS confirmed that this approach was acceptable.

Other known sources of leakage included the two existing front doors, which are joined with an astragal, a molding piece often used as a seal between a pair of doors. The landmark commission would not allow Shannon to replace these older, leaky doors. To reduce the 250 CFM_{50} of leakage through these doors, Shannon hired a custom cabinetmaker to install double gaskets on them.

Once they arrived, the Optiwin windows were installed from the inside, with most set about 3 inches in from the outermost layer of brick. The spray foam that was applied in the rough opening connects behind the framing, which is set off of the brick, to the spray foam on the interior side of the brick, forming a continuous layer. Over that foam, butyl tape was used to adhere the window to the framing,

Shannon took care to preserve many of the original details in the brownstone, including much of its mahogany trim.

A solar thermal system will supply 75% to 80% of the annual demand for hot water.

and standard caulking foam was used to seal any remaining leaks. Brick molding around the windows covers the gap between the window and the brick. The drywall layer was thoroughly sealed with spray foam and standard caulk to form a secondary air barrier.

Three existing fireplaces were masonry sealed to prevent air leakage, rather than being removed, as the clients liked the look of the fireplaces and mantels. Although one of these fireplaces is no longer functional, the fireplace in the main parlor room and the master bedroom have been given second lives, having been retrofitted with EcoSmart fireboxes that burn ethanol cleanly enough that no venting is necessary. The one in the parlor is topped by a beautiful marble mantel and surrounded by mahogany molding and built-in shelves, combining modern technology with Craftsman grace notes.

To bring fresh air into the retrofitted brownstone, Shannon chose not one but two Zehnder ComfoAir 350 HRVs, which have a rated efficiency of 84% at their least efficient point of operation. The 350 was the smallest unit available at the time. He had one installed in the cellar. For now, the cellar has no other air-conditioning system, although Shannon put in an extra refrigerant line, in case the clients feel the need for more cooling there in the summer. The other unit is mounted on the top floor and supplies fresh air to the rest of the building.

To cool the building, and to provide supplemental heat when needed, Shannon is relying on two Daikin mini-split air-to-air heat pump units. The garden apartment has its own wall-mounted ¾-ton unit, while a ceiling-mounted 1½-ton unit conditions the triplex. The one condenser that serves both units is on the roof. This total of 2¼ tons of air-conditioning for the two living spaces stands in sharp contrast to the 7½-ton systems that Shannon has been used to installing in brownstones of this size. Shannon expects the Daikin units to provide good humidity control in summer.

Instead of using Zehnder's proprietary ducts, White designed a custom duct system, which was fabricated by a local HVAC contractor in-house, in order to avoid having separate ductwork for fresh air, heating, and cooling. A backdraft damper located near the HRV opens or closes,

New York City Landmark Commission members were excited about the opportunity this project presented to showcase **preservation efforts that would result in a more-sustainable building**.

depending on whether heating, cooling, or just fresh air is called for.

Unimpressed with what they had read about condensing washer/dryers, the clients chose instead to buy a conventional dryer. Shannon and White accommodated this preference by piping fresh air directly into the laundry room to balance the exhaust requirements of the dryer. The exhaust ductwork runs through the attic insulation, which is dense-packed cellulose, and then out to the roof. A mechanical damper seals off this exhaust duct when the

dryer is not in use. According to the PHPP calculations, this penetration to the outdoors will have only a minimal effect on overall energy loss.

While a house need not generate renewable energy in order to meet the PH standard, a solar-thermal system can greatly reduce overall energy use. Two 4-foot by 10-foot Heliodyne flat-plate collectors, with a Heliopak heat exchanger, will supply 75% to 80% of the hot water annual demand for the two families. The percentage supplied will vary by season, with the solar collectors meeting almost

100% of the summer demand and probably 60% of the winter demand. The collectors were installed at a roughly 20° angle, but with the long side against the roof, in order to meet the landmark commission's visual clearance stipulations. The solar-heated water flows to a 120-gallon storage tank, and then goes for backup heating to a Rinnai on-demand gas condensing water heater, which is 96% efficient. The Rinnai heater only turns on when the water falls below a preset temperature—a triggering mechanism that Shannon looked long and hard to find. All of the other tankless systems that he found operate by a flow sensor, which turns on the heater every time there is a demand for water, whether that demand is for cold or hot water.

Tackling a brownstone retrofit is complicated. It is not a job for the faint of heart, nor for those with tight budgets. But since the cost to redo a townhouse is pretty high no matter what, taking a retrofit to the PH level isn't all that much more expensive. When Shannon analyzed his figures, he calculated that the PH measures increased the cost of the retrofit by 2.7% compared to standard construction. This up-front investment should pay back in six to seven years, for a savings-investment ratio of 5.

The client has agreed to let White and Shannon monitor the building for the next two years. They plan to collect data to (1) determine the output of the solar-thermal panels; (2) measure the temperatures in various rooms and determine the temperature range from room to room; (3) monitor gas usage, especially for the backup water heater; and (4) monitor electricity usage. Periodically they will also run tests to monitor IAQ. Trying to meet the airtightness standard in this building has been very challenging, and as of this writing, it still wasn't clear whether that challenge would be met. One lesson that Shannon learned from this retrofit was not to rely on spray foam insulation to create an air barrier. It's a lesson that he will apply to the next brownstone he works on. Above the cellar walls, he plans to use a StoGuard coating for the air barrier and cellulose—which has a much lower embodied energy than spray foam—for the insulation. He may still need to use spray foam insulation in the cellar, since Brooklyn cellars tend to be wet and spray foam is effective as a moisture barrier, but he is searching for an even better solution.

Although it has been a challenge trying to meet the PH airtightness standard, the building meets both of the other PH standard requirements: the 15 kWh/m² per year for heating energy use and the 120 kWh/m² per year for overall source energy use. The updated brownstone is now a model of energy efficiency and excellent IAQ. Noises from the vibrant Park Slope neighborhood barely register indoors, thanks in large part to the quality of the triple-pane windows. Shannon is deeply appreciative of his clients' commitment to this project—and to their efforts to shrink their family's carbon footprint. His clients, in turn, are thrilled with the performance and beauty of their new home.

PASSIVE HOUSE
Verification Summary

Builder	Jeremy Shannon	**Specific Space Heat Demand**	15 kWh/m²/yr (1.4 kWh/ft²/yr)
PH Consultant	Jeremy Shannon/ David White	**Pressurization Test Result**	0.6 ACH$_{50}$*
Architect	Jeremy Shannon	**Specific Primary Energy Demand** (DHW, Heating, Cooling, Auxiliary, and Household Electricity)	77 kWh/m²/yr (7.1 kWh/ft²/yr)
City	Brooklyn, New York	**Specific Useful Cooling Energy Demand**	8 kWh/m²/yr (0.7 kWh/ft²/yr)
Year	2010		

*target

CHAPTER 10

Updating a California Classic

Larkspur, California

Built just before California's first energy code for homes became law, this early '70s house featured all the hallmarks of that architectural era—large expanses of single-pane windows, vaulted ceilings, wood paneling, and even an avocado-green tub and sink. The very features that gave this house its style when it was built almost 40 years ago are also the ones that made it uncomfortable in winter and summer both.

Nestled at the foot of a small hill, the house is the last one on the street and backs up onto a 300-acre county-owned open space district. Oriented to take full advantage of the woodland scenery, the living room's large aluminum-framed, single-pane windows overlook a sunny vista of redwood, bay, and sycamore trees. East facing, these windows let early-morning light and heat into the room. In summer, the living room and the adjacent, east-facing master bedroom would heat up quickly, and the heat would build throughout the day. By late afternoon, temperatures in these rooms would hit the mid- to high 80s and sometimes even the low 90s. In winter, the heat in the house radiated out through the glass in these windows, whose R-value might have been as high as 1; warm air also escaped through the gap between the window frame and the wall. On cold winter mornings, condensation would bead up on the interior surface of the cold glass, run down the window, and pool on the bottom windowsill.

The vaulted ceiling gives an airy feeling to the modest living room and master bedroom. That design choice, however, means that the house has no attic, where insulation can usually be added to slow heat loss from the living space out through the roof tiles. In winter, because there was no insulation under the roof either, the heat that was pumped into the house from the forced-air heating system rose up toward the ceiling and floated away through every crack and joint in the wood-paneled ceiling. In summer, heat from the sun radiated through the roof tiles and baked the house.

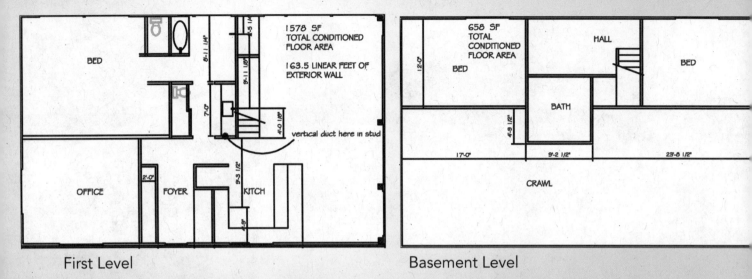

1578 SF
TOTAL CONDITIONED
FLOOR AREA

163.5 LINEAR FEET OF
EXTERIOR WALL

vertical duct here in stud

BED

OFFICE

FOYER

KITCH

658 SF
TOTAL
CONDITIONED
FLOOR AREA

HALL

BED

BATH

BED

17'-0"

9'-2 1/2"

23'-8 1/2"

CRAWL

Another design feature—the living room's pecky-cedar paneling—gave the house the feeling of an Alpine cabin, but it was porous, with little fissures and poorly sealed joints, and warm air migrated through it easily. The redwood siding on the exterior wasn't any more airtight than the interior siding, and with spotty or no insulation in the walls, keeping the house at a comfortable temperature was more of an occasion than an everyday experience.

No easy or inexpensive fixes existed for this house. Adding insulation is generally the first, most cost-effective option to consider when one is trying to cut energy use, or to make a home more comfortable. Not in this case. The usual way to add insulation to an existing wall is to punch small holes in the wall, blow in some insulation, and then patch and repaint the wall. But holes in wood paneling are not easily patched and covered up. With wood paneling on the outside and inside, that option was out. Adding insulation under the roof was out until it was time to reroof. Adding insulation to a wood-paneled, vaulted ceiling would have destroyed its look. Windows can be replaced, but well-built windows are expensive, and new windows alone wouldn't have cut the home's energy use that much. Still, after 20 years of uncomfortable living, it was time for a major change.

Having read about and even visited some Passive Houses, the homeowner knew that she wanted to use the PH approach to remodel her house. She chose to work with Quantum Builders for Sustainable Living, because the owners were already familiar with the PH standard and were reframing their business to emphasize it. At that time, the firm's architect and designer were in the process of training to become PH consultants.

Before jumping into any PH retrofit, the first thing a PH consultant has to decide is where the continuous airtight layer—from the roof to the foundation—is going to be. It is always challenging to create a continuous airtight layer in a retrofit—usually much more challenging than to do so in new construction, as existing features can interfere with the continuity of an airtight layer. In this house, the walls were going to need a major overhaul to make them airtight. This task could be tackled either from the outside or from the inside. The homeowner decided that the best approach would be to rebuild the walls from the outside, since this would cost less and would be easier to live through. The existing exterior siding—made from redwood plywood— would become the airtight layer, and this layer would be made continuous by carefully sealing the joints between the redwood panels, between the walls and the roof deck, and

The walls were rebuilt from the outside, making the retrofit process easier to live through.

between the wall and the concrete foundation. To complete the wall overhaul and to increase the wall's R-value, the old siding would then be covered over with a layer of insulation, a rain screen, and new siding.

Generally, architects and builders of older homes gave very little thought to airtightness. That was certainly the case in this house. The first blower door test, before any work was done, came in at a horribly leaky 3,500 CFM_{50}. Hitting the PH airtightness performance target would require reducing this leakiness by 1,400%—to 250 CFM_{50}. Many contractors would have refused to accept a challenge like that. However, Quantum Builders' Project Manager, Carlos Velasquez, and his crew tackled the task enthusiastically.

Air sealing the topmost layer of this house from the inside would have been quite complicated, what with the vaulted ceilings. Fortunately that challenge could be sidestepped, since the existing asphalt-tiled roof was nearing the end of its useful life anyway. Tearing off the old

roof would grant access to the roof deck, which the crew could then seal. To keep the total costs down, the architect, Josh Moore, searched for a cost-effective roof replacement that would also increase the R-value of the roof assembly. Moore recommended installing a product that is more commonly found on commercial roofs, a metal structural insulated panel (SIP). The Kingspan SIP that was chosen uses foamed-in-place urethane-modified isocyanurate for the insulation layer and comes prefinished with a standing-seam metal cladding, which serves as the roof exterior finish. The 6-inch-thick SIP delivers an R-value of 49, and is fire resistant to boot—an important characteristic for a house that sits on the border of a heavily wooded open space district. Metal roofs come in a variety of colors; to decrease the heat absorption through the roof, the homeowner chose white, since it is highly reflective. For this roof the solar reflectance index (SRI), which assesses a material's ability to reject solar heat, is 85 on a scale where black rates 0 and white rates 100.

After removing the old asphalt tiles, Velasquez and his crew covered the roof sheathing in plywood and carefully air sealed it at every juncture with a flexible waterproofing material called Sto Gold Coat. The joint between the plywood decking and the existing walls was thoroughly sealed with the same product, as was all of the exterior siding. All junctures between the plywood sheets were sealed with Sto, as were nail holes and other small breaches in the façade. Larger holes, such as penetrations for exterior lighting, were foamed over.

Several years earlier, the homeowner had had the crawl space sealed to reduce moisture migration from the soil into the house. A vapor barrier had been laid over the dirt floor and then run up and taped to the walls. However, no attempt had been made to seal the crawl space completely; penetrations for wiring and pipes were not foamed, and several vents were left open, as was then required by the building code. One gas-fired appliance remained in the crawl space—an on-demand water heater, which was direct-vented through the crawl space wall.

To create a truly continuous air barrier, the crawl space had to be completely sealed, and the joint between the foundation and the walls had to be sealed, too. But first, the construction crew worked to insulate the foundation from the ground. They began by digging a 2-foot trench all the way around the concrete foundation. Drainage mat was put in where none existed. Then the crew installed a 2-inch-thick block of EPS all around the outside of the foundation. The water heater was moved outdoors to eliminate the hole through the envelope needed for the exhaust vent, and to do away with any possibility of carbon monoxide (CO) poisoning. All of the smaller envelope penetrations were sealed with Sto, and a continuous coat of this sealant was used to close up the joint between the concrete foundation and the redwood siding.

Making an existing house extremely airtight is a persnickety task that requires a dedicated and professional crew. The right tool also helps. For this task, that tool was a blower door, which the general contractor used daily for about ten days to pressurize the house. While the fan was pumping air into the house, his crew would walk around outside, feeling for any air movement that would indicate smaller and still smaller penetrations.

Creating the continuous airtight layer required several design changes, some of which were problematic for the homeowner. Fireplaces and their chimneys create large holes in the exterior envelope, which are very difficult to seal properly. Since fireplaces are notorious for losing heat up the chimney, the homeowner somewhat reluctantly agreed to take out the fireplace and the chimney vent altogether and seal up the resulting gap with plywood and Sto. Another hole that created difficulty was the dryer vent. Passive Houses in Europe are seldom equipped with dryers that need to be vented. Instead, people use condensing dryers or drying closets to remove the moisture from

Hitting the airtightness target required reducing the leakiness of this home by 1,400%.

clothes. After debating various options, the homeowner chose to move the washer and dryer to the garage.

The amenity that was the most difficult to sacrifice was the skylights. No skylights can provide the R-value equivalent of a roof overhead. Rather, they tend to act as chimney vents, drawing the heat up and out of the house. The homeowner struggled to choose between enjoying more natural light in winter and reducing heat loss. The latter won out, and the skylights were removed.

As soon as the house was air sealed, it felt dramatically different. For the first time, cold drafts didn't sweep through the house. The temperature inside held steady for much longer than it ever had before. This change became even more noticeable as the single-pane windows were swapped out. After considering several high-performance

The new roof, constructed with a 6-inch-thick structural insulated panel, delivers an R-value of 49 and keeps the heat out of the house on even the hottest of days.

models, the homeowner finally chose Sorpetaler's wood-framed, argon-filled, triple-pane windows. She selected a mix of fixed and operable windows to replace her old sliders. The operable ones have a tilt-and-turn mechanism; they can be tilted open to provide a little ventilation, or swung wide to provide full ventilation. Adjustable multipoint fittings ensure a very tight seal when the windows are closed. The glazing has an R-value of 7; the SHGC for these windows is .50.

To protect the new windows from moisture, and to eliminate even minimal air leakage, Velasquez set up a triple line of defense around the windows. First, he installed flashing over the studs that form the window opening. Then he installed double-sided Tyvek flashing, which has adhesive on both sides, with one side glued to the window frame and the other side glued to the house framing. Finally, he installed another layer of Tyvek over the window frame and the window opening on the outside of the house. This last layer was sealed to the original redwood siding to ensure a continuous airtight boundary.

When all 12 windows and the four doors had been replaced, and the air sealing was finished, the house felt solid for the first time. The walls were finally performing their intended function, creating a barrier between outdoors and indoors. Thanks to the crew's persistent and thorough efforts, the final blower door test came in at 225 CFM_{50}—surpassing the PH target of 250 CFM_{50}. This was truly a cause for celebration for the whole crew. As far as anyone knew, it was the first time in the United States that a retrofit had met the airtightness requirement of the PH standard.

Velasquez next turned his crew to thickening up the walls. He began by adding 3 inches of Roxul's rigid mineral wool insulation. The homeowner chose this product because it has a lower environmental impact than foam does. Unlike foam, it is not petroleum derived; it is made from volcanic rock and slag, a waste product. It is water and fire resistant, and it has a minimum of 40% recycled content. The rigid insulation, which is held in place by 3-inch washers and 5-inch-long screws at each corner of the 2-foot by 4-foot sheets, has an R-value of 14. A crinkly Tyvek drain wrap covers the mineral wool and serves as a rain screen. Over the drain wrap are wooden battens, held in place by 6-inch-long screws set into the studs. Fiber cement siding, chosen for its durability, forms the outermost layer. A ¾-inch air gap remains between

Although temperatures slid into the 30s at night, **the house was snug for the first time ever**. No drafts chilled the air. The inside surface of the new windows was much warmer to the touch than the old aluminum sliders had been.

the siding and the drain wrap, so that any rain that penetrates the siding will run down the wrap and drip out of the assembly.

As the house became more and more airtight, the homeowner began for the first time to use the ventilation system. She had had the system installed two years earlier when she was replacing an older furnace, in anticipation of tightening up her house eventually. The Lifebreath air handler unit includes an HRV with a variable-speed motor that draws air through the system at a low speed when the unit is in ventilation-only mode, or at high speed when it is in heating mode. The Lifebreath HRV does not meet the 80% heat recovery efficiency required for a PH, but since this piece of equipment was installed relatively recently, the homeowner elected to keep it in place, rather than replace it with a compliant unit.

When heat is needed, the supply air is warmed up by a water-to-air heat exchanger. Hot water is provided by a solar-thermal system, backed up by an on-demand water heater. A 2kW PV system generates electricity that helps meet the home's overall energy demand.

Costs for the remodel totaled up at about $140/ft^2$. That is expensive for a retrofit, but the exterior walls were essentially rebuilt, and the roof was replaced. The quality of the products used should preclude the need for any major repairs for 40 years.

Modeling this home with the PHPP software, it became clear that, even after the retrofit, the house would not meet the PH heating energy demand requirement. This requirement could be met in the PHPP by adding a layer of foam insulation on the bottom floor to insulate it from the ground and prevent heat loss there. The cost of this improvement exceeded the homeowner's present budget; she hopes to add the insulation in the future. Quantum Builders consider this project to be a prototype for a phased PH retrofit, in which the PHPP is used as a tool to plan and implement a strategic renovation. With this approach, it is critical to ensure that all of the work that gets done contributes to the goal of a PH retrofit, and that no components or installation techniques will need to be replaced or redone for at least another 20 years.

Winter arrived just as the crew were putting the finishing coat of paint on the new siding. Although temperatures slid into the 30s at night, the house was snug for the first time ever. No drafts chilled the air. The inside surface of the new windows was much warmer to the touch than the old aluminum sliders had been. Guided by the PH approach, a dedicated crew had transformed a drafty house into an inviting, comfortable home.

PASSIVE HOUSE
Verification Summary

Builder	Quantum Builders for Sustainable Living	Specific Space Heat Demand	4.58 kBtu/ft²/yr (1.3 kWh/ft²/yr)*
PH Consultant	Mary Graham	Pressurization Test Result	0.54 ACH$_{50}$
Architect	Josh Moore	Specific Primary Energy Demand (DHW, Heating, Cooling, Auxiliary, and Household Electricity)	34.7 kBtu/ft²/yr* (10.2 kWh/ft²/yr)*
City	Larkspur, California		
Year	2010	Specific Useful Cooling Energy Demand	4.75 kBtu/ft²yr (1.4 kWh/ft²/yr)*

*when project is completed

CHAPTER 11

The First **Modular** Passive House

Charlotte, Vermont

A sketch created during a conference session seems an unlikely candidate for the birth of a small revolution—the first modular Passive House in North America—but no matter what its origins, it's a birth that deserves celebration. Architect J.B. Clancy and Peter Schneider, project manager and energy analyst with Vermont Energy Investment Corporation—both are also PH consultants—were conferring at the 2009 North American Passive House Conference. Schneider had heard that Habitat for Humanity was planning to build three homes on a $1/2$-acre section of a 50-acre parcel in his hometown of Charlotte, Vermont.

He knew that Habitat was becoming increasingly interested in energy efficiency, and that for this project the organization was planning to add donated rigid foam to the outside of the building shell. He figured pushing Habitat's design to meet the PH standard wouldn't be too difficult or too expensive. When he approached the executive director of Habitat's local chapter, Green Mountain Habitat, with this suggestion, it was welcomed enthusiastically. But the original design—a traditional Cape-style home—was overcomplicated and would need to be modified. That's where Clancy came in.

Clancy and Schneider had met during the PH consultant training in the spring and early summer of 2009. Before that, Clancy had had plenty of experience with green building standards, but he wasn't satisfied with getting points awarded for specifying the installation of bamboo flooring imported from China. How was that really reducing a home's environmental footprint? Dissatisfied and searching for a standard that would focus on energy efficiency, he found the PH consultant training. Several months later, he was happy to apply what he had learned in the classroom to the Habitat project. Then and there, Clancy sketched up a design for a small, cost-effective PH that could be either stick-built or modular housing. That basic design never changed much. As Schneider says, it was an incredibly efficient and buildable design.

Habitat for Humanity builds affordable housing for families who are earning 30% of the area's median income

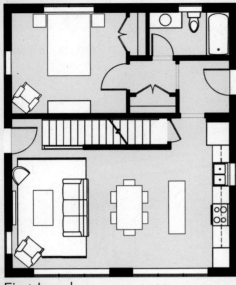

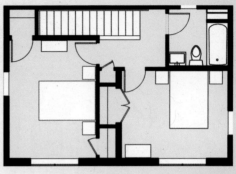

Second Level

First Level

or less and are currently in insufficient housing. It is very competitive to get into one of Habitat's houses, and once in, the families tend to stay for decades. In the Northeast, Habitat understands that affordability doesn't just mean low initial costs or monthly mortgages. Affordability includes life cycle costs, especially energy costs. Being able to control the home's energy costs, and protect the homeowner from future cost increases, is what makes housing affordable in the long term.

That control was what made PH interesting to David Mullin, the executive director of Green Mountain Habitat. The clincher was the cost analysis prepared by Schneider and Clancy. They used the PHPP to chart monthly energy use in their PH design compared to a traditional Cape-style home, and then translated that energy use into monthly energy costs. The increased costs to build the PH, and the resulting higher mortgage bill, were more than offset by the savings in energy costs, even if Habitat had to pay for more insulation and the upgraded windows. If Habitat invested in building a PH now, the new owner would save money immediately.

Charlotte, Vermont, is a small town of roughly 4,000, tucked away in the northwestern corner of Vermont, just 10 miles south of Burlington. Because the Burlington area is extremely cloudy, and because there are a great many

heating degree-days per year, this is arguably one of the most challenging climates in the United States in which to build a PH. And yet. And still. Even here, a cost-effective PH is possible.

What's the secret? Schneider cites the simplicity of the design, a modular building approach, utilizing products available in North America, and then stops himself. Most important, he says, is using smart design to decrease the size of the house and still meet all the requirements of an average family. The final design has 1,375 square feet of living space and a very smart floor plan. On the first floor, the kitchen, dining room, and living room flow seamlessly together, occupying one-half of the downstairs. A master bedroom, bath, and mudroom occupy the other half. Upstairs, two more bedrooms share a full bath on a floor that is roughly two-thirds as wide as the first floor. A shaded porch area frames the west-facing front door.

The level of detail that the PHPP requires is what makes this modeling tool particularly practical. Without this tool, says Clancy, what passes for a studied design choice is really just shooting from the hip. Using the PHPP, Clancy was able to design a home in which passive solar is providing two-thirds of the heat load, even though Vermont is the second-cloudiest state in the nation. As Schneider says, it's

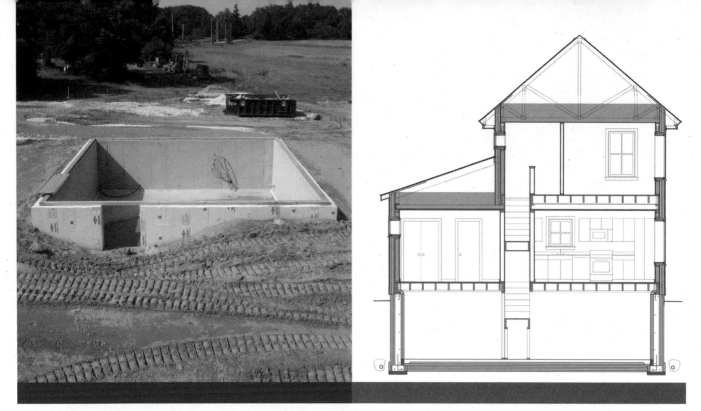

The foundation wall is wrapped on the outside with 6 inches of XPS, while the interior of the foundation walls is covered in two 2-inch layers of polyisocyanurate.

pretty remarkable what the sun can provide, even in a poor solar climate.

Habitat's first PH could have been stick-built or modular housing, but Mullin understood that a modular PH could be replicated more easily on the open market. And a model that could be easily replicated would give more families a shot at living in a comfortable, superefficient home. Early in the planning process, after Schneider had given a talk at a building conference about the Habitat project, Dave Stewart and Chet Pasho of Preferred Building Systems (PBS) approached him, proposing to collaborate on the project. PBS is currently a leader in energy-efficient modular homes; this project would be an upgrade from its existing, highly efficient construction practices. Under ordinary market rate conditions, modular homes are less costly to construct than stick-built ones, but Habitat homes are built with volunteer labor—a cost savings that PBS just couldn't match. Instead, it could and did offer to shave its costs as much as possible in order to get this project built. Schneider successfully closed the remaining budget

gap with additional fund-raising from local philanthropic organizations.

The exterior wall components, which were built in the PBS factory, are constructed with 2 x 6 engineered studs at 24 inches OC and single top plates, an advanced framing design that reduces the amount of wood used and allows for the installation of relatively more cellulose insulation. Over the framing members, a Huber ZIP System, which consists of structural panels with a built-in water-resistant barrier and a proprietary tape to seal the seams, provides a combined sheathing and air barrier layer. This ZIP system was used to form the exterior walls and the roof sheathing. The roof design, with its 20-inch raised-heel truss, allows for a generously proportioned attic that is filled with 2 feet of cellulose, giving the roof assembly an R-value of approximately 90.

Three 2-inch boards of foil-faced polyisocyanurate rigid foam, layered on with staggered seams, wrap the above-grade walls. That foam is held on with wood strapping. Screws that go all the way back through the foam to the

The modular-home components were built in the Preferred Building Systems factory.

studs hold the strapping in place, and the siding is attached to the strapping. Since Schneider and Clancy are choosing cement board for the siding, and since cement board is heavier than other types of siding and doesn't travel as well, it will be attached on site. The total R-value of the exterior walls is 60.

For the windows, Schneider chose to have PBS install Thermotech 332 Gain+ units, which have a glass and frame U-value of .16 and a spacer U-value of .024. The SHGC is .64, the highest value they could find. They used casements on the east and west sides, and awning-style windows on the north side. On the south side, fixed-pane windows are mulled to casements on both sides. These triple-pane windows come with slim, well-insulated, fiberglass frames.

As this book went to press, Schneider and Clancy were eagerly awaiting the imminent delivery of the modular-home components. All of the site preparation and below-grade construction had been finished. The footings, which extend 4 feet below the frost line, sit on and are wrapped in 4 inches of XPS. The one load-bearing footing in the center

of the 4-inch concrete slab is similarly wrapped in foam. Buried beneath the slab are six layers of 2-inch XPS boards with staggered seams, for a total of 12 inches of foam. The foundation wall is wrapped on the outside with 6 inches of XPS, while the interior of the foundation walls is covered in two 2-inch layers of polyisocyanurate.

The modular-home components will be assembled on site by a PBS set crew. The finish details will be completed using an all-volunteer crew, as is true of all Habitat homes. In some locations, an all-volunteer crew can be a mixed blessing, with enthusiastic but unskilled volunteers. That won't be the case in Charlotte, where local carpenters have volunteered to pitch in, trading free labor for the experience of helping to construct a PH.

The volunteers will be responsible for all interior and exterior finishes, including trim, flooring, cabinetry, and siding, and for installing the asphalt shingles on the roof. In addition, although the ducts and rough wiring and plumbing were included in the wall components, the mechanical system will be installed on site.

To meet the home's heating load and supply fresh air, Schneider opted for an UltimateAir ERV with a rated efficiency of 83%. He also specified installing a water-to-air coil that preheats the incoming air. The liquid in the coil is actually a water-glycol mix that runs through a double loop of standard PEX tubing, which was installed around the home's footing. In Charlotte, the ground temperature below the frost line is typically 50°F. The tubing transfers the earth's heat to the water-glycol mix, boosting the temperature of the outside air when it is 10°F or colder by about 40°F. This preheating also prevents very cold outdoor air from damaging the ERV. This relatively inexpensive system is completely passive, except for a 30W circulator pump tied to a temperature sensor that measures the incoming air. The rest of the heating load will be supplied with a 12,000 Btu air-to-air source heat pump, manufactured by Mitsubishi. This unit provides a 100% output at 5°F and a 75% output at -13°F; and it shuts off at -18°F.

The cooling load—well, that's not really a problem in Vermont. Neither is humidity. While summertime weather rarely amounts to much of a challenge, there are a few weeks when the heat and humidity can get uncomfortable—but that same 50°F liquid is still circulating through the coil. In summer, that liquid can precool the incoming air by condensing out excess moisture, which then gets dumped through a condensate drain. Combine that strategy with night cooling—closing the house during the day and opening it up at night—and those few weeks of summer heat can be enjoyed very comfortably.

Shading is also unnecessary here. According to the PHPP modeling results, even eliminating the overhangs on the south-facing windows will not overheat the house. On peak cooling days, the sun is at a 23° angle, way up in the center of the sky, and the high-performance windows reflect most of the heat. In the late spring and early fall, when it is still, or already, the heating season, the absence of overhangs lets in more solar heat. Averaged over the year, the eyebrowless look lowers energy consumption.

In spite of Vermont's solar limitations, Schneider calculated that a solar water heater should provide 75% of the annual DHW load. He chose to install a flat, black, closed-loop system with a water-glycol mix, and an 80-gallon storage tank. A well-insulated 40-gallon electric water heater will serve as backup.

Schneider and Clancy's goal was to keep the home's systems as simple as possible, and to minimize maintenance for the occupants. Although they generally succeeded, the systems in a PH are often unfamiliar to the homeowner. To ease the transition, Schneider and Clancy plan to conduct

The positive response to this product shouldn't be surprising, given that **choosing a modular home considerably shortens the time it takes to build a certified PH and minimizes the budgetary uncertainties** that can arise during a home-building project.

training and postoccupancy evaluations every three months for the first year. They will also offer a five-year maintenance contract to make sure everything is being maintained appropriately.

For Habitat, the price to deliver the modular PH package will be $100/ft², but that doesn't include the mechanical system, asphalt roofing, or finish flooring. With site work and a foundation, but not counting the price of the land, this package will cost just over $115/ft². Include the mechanical system and the finish flooring, and the total cost for a complete house would be $130/ft². That price compares amazingly well with what it costs to get a custom house built almost anywhere in the United States, and certainly in Vermont, where labor costs are high. A custom house usually goes for somewhere in the high $100s to $200/ft².

This efficient and buildable design, which has been precertified by PHIUS, is now available as a PH modular home from PBS. PBS can deliver its modular-home components to any site in the New England region. When this modular PH is assembled in a different location, the climate data will have to be updated to reflect that location, but as long as the due south orientation is preserved and the solar access is good, the modular home should meet the PH requirements. Depending on where the home will be sited, the shading system might have to be adjusted. Cost for this modular PH would be from $130 to $150/ft², depending on the choice of finishes and siding, as well as the distance from the PBS factory to the site. Once a contract with PBS is signed and all the final design decisions have been made, it should take no longer than eight weeks to assemble and deliver the home components, according to Stewart.

PBS has already received many inquiries about its new modular PH, and as this book went to press, one new order was already in the works. The positive response to this product shouldn't be surprising, given that choosing a modular home considerably shortens the time it takes to build a certified PH and minimizes the budgetary uncertainties that can arise during a home-building project. Streamlining access to a PH may not be a dramatic revolution, but sharply reducing carbon emissions in the housing industry doesn't call for drama—just action. Innovation doesn't hurt, either.

PASSIVE HOUSE
Verification Summary

Builder	Habitat for Humanity	Specific Space Heat Demand	4.63 kBtu/ft²/yr (1.4 kWh/ft²/yr)
PH Consultant	Peter Schneider/ J.B. Clancy	Pressurization Test Result	0.6 ACH_{50}*
Architect	J.B. Clancy	Specific Primary Energy Demand (DHW, Heating, Cooling, Auxiliary, and Household Electricity)	36 kBtu/ft²/yr (10.6 kWh/ft²/yr)
City	Charlotte, Vermont	Specific Useful Cooling Energy Demand	3 kBtu/ft²/yr (0.9 kWh/ft²/yr)
Year	2010		

*target

Visit Us **Online**

For more information on these and other Passive House projects, visit
lowcarbonproductions.com.

Glossary-Index

Photo **Credits**

Foreword
p. i Courtesy of Jonah Stanford

Chapter 1: Introduction
p. 3 Adam Fagen
p. 4 Mary James
p. 5 Chris Benedict
p. 6 Joel Bernstein
p. 7 Adam Bell

Chapter 2: The Steamy Side of Passive House
All photos by Corey Saft

Chapter 3: A Home for Their Future
pp. 17, 20-21 Blake Bilyeu
p. 22 Sarah Evans

Chapter 4: A Wine Country Retrofit
All photos by Solar Knights Construction

Chapter 5: PH in the High Desert: The Breezeway House
All photos by Jeremy Wold

Chapter 6: The Passive House in the Woods
All photos by Tim Eian

Chapter 7: A Community Effort Creates Affordable Housing
All photos by Joel Bernstein, except p. 51 photo by Terry Nordbye

Chapter 8: Transforming a Family Home
All photos by Tad Everhart, except p. 66 Robin Cassatt-Johnstone

Chapter 9: Sustainability and Preservation—Twin Goals for a Retrofit
All photos by Adam Bell

Chapter 10: Updating a California Classic
pp. 75, 77, 80 Rolf Schulz
pp. 78, 79 Keith Ovregaard

Chapter 11: The First Modular Passive House
pp. 85, 88 Peter Schneider
p. 86 courtesy of Preferred Building Systems

Author Bio
p. 98 Joel Bernstein

Resources

CALIFORNIA

Beyond Efficiency

Katy Hollbacher
Berkeley, CA and Jackson, NY
www.beyondefficiency.org
(415)236-1333
one-stop technical consulting for PH architects

Integral Impact Inc

Prudence Ferreira
San Francisco, CA
(415)516-1368
pf@integralimpactinc.com
www.integralimpactinc.com

Sunset Screens

Jeff Kamariotis
Marin County, CA
www.sunsetscreens.com
(415)652-6615
authorized phantom screen dealer

Solar Knights Construction

Rick Milburn
Napa, CA
www.solar-knights.com
(707)975-6912

Sylvia Wallis Architecture

Sylvia Wallis
Los Angeles, CA
liweiya@sbcglobal.net
(213)453-8071
PH design, consulting and energy modeling

Tektive Design

Pearl Renaker
Palo Alto, CA
www.tektivedesign.com
(415)250-6052
PH consultant and designer

MASSACHUSETTS

The DEAP Energy Group, LLC

Mike Duclos, Paul Eldrenkamp,
Paul Panish
Boston, MA
www.deapgroup.com
(617)775-4716
design and construction of PH and other extremely efficient homes

ZeroEnergy Design

Stephanie Horowitz
Boston, MA
www.zeroenergy.com
(617)720-5002
Architecture, HVAC Design, PH Consulting

MICHIGAN

Freedom Pet Pass Pet Door Company

Brian Algar
Bay City, MI
www.freedompetpass.com
(989)667-3763
airtight pet doors (see chapter 3)

Sturgeon Bay Woodworks, Inc

Steven Johnston
Harbor Springs, MI
steve@passivehousenorth.com
(231)838-6432
Design/Build Construction Services, PH Consultant

MINNESOTA

COULSON

Carly Coulson
Duluth, MN
www.carlycoulson.com
(612)384-8661
Architects and PH Consultants

M.C. Howard Builders Corp.

Matt Howard
Two Harbors, MN
mchoward@mac.com
www.mchowardbuilders.com
(612)280-3067

Peak Building Products, LLC

Stephan Tanner
Watertown, MN
www.peakbp.net
(651)925-0866
PH products; Optiwin, Vacupor, Luefta, InnoFlex, Agepan

Optiwin-USA, LLC

Stephan Tanner
Watertown, MN
www.optiwin-usa.com
(651)925-0866
Alu2Wood, 3Wood windows and patio doors, Frostkorken entry doors

TE Studio Limited

Tim Delhey Eian
Minneapolis, MN
info@testudio.com
(612)246-4670
residential PH design experts

NEW HAMPSHIRE

RH Irving Homebuilders

Bob Irving
Salisbury, NH
www.rhirvinghomebuilders.com
(603)648-2635
PH consultant and home builder specializing in low energy homes

NEW JERSEY

Energy Works, LLC

Christine Liaukus
Bloomfield, NJ
www.energyworksnj.com
(201)704-0844
PH design/consulting, residential design/build, energy audits

NEW YORK

Charles Lauster Architect, P.C.

Peter Kincl
New York, NY
pkincl@lausterarchitect.com
lausterarchitect.com
(212)679-1110

Gifford Fuel Savings

Henry Gifford/Chris Benedict
New York, NY
Henry@EnergySavingScience.com
(212)477-6016
over 75 no-extra-cost, very energy efficient buildings designed so far

Jill Porter, Architect

Jill Porter
Brooklyn, NY
www.porter-arch.com

Tiptoe Energy

Mary Graham
Trumansburg, NY
mary@TiptoeEnergy.com
energy modeling, design consultation, certification management

ZeroEnergy Design

Jordan Goldman
Brooklyn, NY
www.zeroenergy.com
(617)720-5002
Architecture, HVAC Design, PH Consulting

OHIO

Path 2 Passive House

Edwin Shank
Berea, OH
www.Path2PassiveHouse.com
(216)276-1205
PH consultant, mechanical systems design, SketchUp 3-D modeling

UltimateAir Inc

Jason Morosko
Athens, OH
jmorosko@ultimateair.com
www.ultimateair.com
(740)594-2277
manufacturer of highly efficient ERVs

OREGON

Green Hammer, Inc.

Stephen Aiguier
Portland, OR
info@greenhammer.com
www.greenhammer.com
(503)804-1746
design-build-energy

Root Design Build

Milos Jovanovic
Portland, OR
www.rootdesignbuild.com
(503)944-9202
sustainable design and construction

Studio-E Architecture pc

Jan Fillinger
Eugene, OR
jan.c.fillinger@gmail.com
www.studio-e-architecture.com
(541)338-7558

Wright On Sustainability

Graham Wright
Portland, OR
graham@wrightonsustainability.com
WrightOnSustainability.com
(503)887-7028

PENNSYLVANNIA

GreenSteps

Laura Blau
Philadelphia, PA
info@greenstepsonline.us
www.greenstepsonline.us
(267)519-3564
PH consulting, sustainable building, and design consulting

UTAH

Coalesce Inc.

Bill Arthur
Salt Lake City, UT
bill@coalescearchitecture.com
www.coalescearchitecture.com
(801)718-5898

VIRGINIA

Peabody Architects

David Peabody
Alexandria , VA
david@greenhaus.org
www.greenhaus.org
(703)684-1986
see the first PH in the DC Metro area at www.greenhaus.org/ blog/

Structures Design Build

Adam Cohen
Roanoke, VA
acohen@structuresdb.com
www.structuresdb.com
(540)774-4800

WASHINGTON

The Artisans Group

Tessa Smith
Olympia, WA
www.artisansgroup.com
(360)570-0626
*design, build energy-efficient
new home or remodel,
certified PH*

BLIP Design

Jim Burton
Seattle, WA
burtonj530@aol.com
(206)501-8746
www.blipdesign.com
green design, PH consulting

Robert Moore, Architect

Robert Moore
Bainbridge Island, WA
www.robertmoorearch.com
(206)842-6366

Stylo Design Studio

Lipika Mukerji
Seattle, WA
lipika@stylostudios.com
www.stylostudios.com
*architecture & sustainable design
services*

Terrapin Architecture, P.C.

Jesse Thomas
Port Townsend, WA
jesse@terrapin-arch.com
terrapinarchitecture.com
(360)379-8090

About the **Author**

Mary James is the editor and publisher at Low Carbon Productions. In 2008, she coauthored *Homes for a Changing Climate: Passive Houses in the U.S.* with Katrin Klingenberg and Mike Kernagis. She was the editor and publisher of *Home Energy* magazine for 10 years. She lives in Northern California with her two children and her dog, Loki.